PreacherWoman for the Goddess

PreacherWoman
for the Goddess

Poems, Invocations, Plays and Other Holy Writ

Bethroot Gwynn

Mother Tongue Ink

www.wemoon.ws
wholesale: 503-288-3588
retail: 1-877-693-6666 or
541-479-4056
P.O. Box 187, Wolf Creek, OR 97497
mothertongue@wemoon.ws

PreacherWoman for the Goddess:
Poems, Invocations, Plays and Other Holy Writ
by Bethroot Gwynn
ISBN: 978-1-942775-12-6
Library of Congress control number: 2017909555
Women's Studies, Earth-Based Spirituality,
Goddess, Feminism, Poetry, Women's Theater

Front cover art: Dancing with Lightning © Deshria 2006
Front cover graphic design artist: Sequoia Watterson
Back cover photo: © Hawk Madrone 2017

Printed in South Korea by Sung In Printing America
on recycled paper using soy based inks.

Mother Tongue Ink publications feature creative work by women,
celebrating earth-based spirituality and visions for a changing
world. Since 1981, MT Ink has published We'Moon: Gaia
Rhythms for Womyn—the iconic astrological datebook, moon
calendar and daily guide to natural cycles—with art and writing
from the growing edge of international women's cultures.

For all the women—across millennia—
who proclaimed Female Sacred
and sang Her praises

For all the women
who would have been comforted
to find Her Holiness in themselves

For all the women
who adore Her creation
enact Her compassions
gladly say Her names
and hear echoes of their own

Contents

She Comes for Us

World Without End

Magic Acts

After

Introduction

Preacher Woman? for the Goddess ? ? ?

I come from a line of back-country Protestant ministers, and something in the inheritance must have stuck because I wound up in theological seminary in the mid-1960s—drawn to passionate conversations about the great Life/Death questions and the socio-political revolutions at hand. But when my revolution came—the Lesbian-Feminist one—I was done with patriarchal religions. I was on fire with female-centered spirituality, and joined other women to create women's lands as Sanctuary for empowerment and imagination; to make art, culture and community devoted to a spirited embrace of earth-life and celebrating the Female as Holy. The domination of divine metaphor by male deity was Over!

There is no simple switch here from patriarchal God to a matriarchal version of Chief Deity. We can play with the ancient honorifics like Queen of Heaven, but feminists usually resist hierarchy. Goddess. Make that Goddesses. Try lower case "g": goddess. In theological terms, we veer toward immanence: divine spirit infuses all existence—the far reaches of cosmos, the inner quantum depths, the immaterial mysteries of consciousness, time, energy. And when we reach for imagery to reflect the Inexpressible, it is high time we look into the mirror. There you are. There I am. All the varieties of us. Woman. Holy.

No construct of gender is able to capture divine essence. But now that the divine genie is released from the bottle of male definition, after centuries of invisibility most especially in Western cultures, Watch Out! She soars, She flexes Her She-muscles, as do we.

These writings are a harvest of 43 years as a back-country "performer" of personal story and poetic musings, and as a student and celebrant of goddess-lore. The work is organized into six sections, each introduced by an Invocation page from a We'Moon Datebook, with poetry and companioning art. Invocation: prayer that summons. I wrote these prayers to invoke the wondrous variety of Goddess energies from many cultures and epochs, calling their power into We'Moon's inspired guidance for these magical but troubled times. Goddess names spill out from these pages, a smattering from the vast worldwide reservoir of divine female images. Blessed be.

1

O Goddesses of The Great Round!
Gaia, Mother Nature, Changing Woman
We are in awe of your mighty spinning
Your Great Cycles of Life/Death/Rebirth
Up and Down and Around
Fortuna and Tyche—Mothers of Destiny
Norns and Moerae—The Three Fates
Arianrhod—Keeper of the Silver Star-Wheel
Kali—Time Dancer, Goddess of the Karmic Wheel
Help us repair the world
Reinvent the human spin
Even as we swing round toward the unthinkable
Help us to trust in your Wholeness.

Invocation for We'Moon 2010: Reinvent the Wheel

In the Lap of the Mother

Nehiyaw Medicine © *Leah Marie Dorion 2005*

Night Song

Full Moon
Full voice
1 a.m. On my deck, alone with sky.
"Where I am is holy
Holy is the ground . . ."
No one around for miles
I hurl my voice to the hills
Rare serenade
"Forest, mountain, river
Listen to the sound
of Great Mother circling
all around . . ."
Echo plays hard to get
I leave off words, hoot my aria

Then I hear them.
Rare serenade
sudden high-pitched howl
almost scream becoming
yip yip yip yip yip
I must have waked them
Will they sing with me?
Quiet. I woman-howl again,
stop, wait
"Great Mother circling. . ."
They chorus back to me
excited cries and yips
conversation   antiphony
I am speaking coyote this night
My call goes out again
That's enough, they say.
Quiet.
We all listen—woman and pups and moon—
"Great Mother circling
all around
here."

Volcano Prayer

All right, Helen. Holy Helen. Saint Helen.
I too, a Helen.
I have clamored for She-gods.
And here you are. Tracing ash trails on green lilac leaves.
Dancing epiphany with an entire region . . .
I take you personally. I admit:
Sometimes the tears insist, like magma they will not stop
    hot molten sadness boils over the rim
    sending up columns of brain tissue cloud.
Sometimes I explode, I do understand.

      Namesake beauty, namesake terror,
      Is it with you as with me?
      Eruption subsided, pressure relieved,
          faced with clean-up, damage repair,
          the asking of forgiveness.
          do I hear your remorse?
          sixty-five dead or missing
          the forest creatures driven dead or mad.

They say you may not be done.
They say the moon may pull your tides of fire again.
Your message is clear: the planet is in charge.
I am willing to beg—
Leave us be now.
Your holiness is without doubt
You are the most lively of saints
Beatified surprise.
You are your own rumbling temple
And we are full of awe.

as Mount St. Helens erupted in 1980

Dry Winter

It has come to this:
I am thrilled to see, at last,
this three-inch slug on my path
this khaki-colored slime creature.
Oh slime! Where have you been,
you and all your relations?
Ah moss! I miss soggy moss
in all her luscious greens.
Where, oh where is mud?
I long for damp.

Last night the sheen of wet
city streets
gave me comfort.
Oh yes, *this* is Oregon!
This is Winter, as it should be.
The dry, the bright blue sky days
have stretched so long
too much is enough
to seize the region with fear
of a tinder brittle summer.
My prayers to keep lightning away
begin already.
I learn,
in these peculiar globe-warm months,
how deep is my love
for the dripping, the pelting
the green-making rain
I pray you Rain
I pray you slugs moss mud
yea, even rot
Come, be wet with us now.

Landed

Still.

The night is so Still. The quiet so profound—I can hear the occasional crisp leaf land in the brush, hear a sweet pea pod snap open. Bugs fiddle a distant chorus of legs. If I listen long enough, a deer will crunch crunch through dry forest; an owl will hoo hoo. Night sky is so available, arching deep dark over trees, ridges, creatures, me. Lavish with stars, clouds of light float a milky way. There is a song we sing, we lesbians:

> *There is a sacred one inside*
> *All the stars and all the galaxies*
> *Run through Her hands like beads.*
> (*Lesbian Circle song, from Sufi tradition*)

I moved to the woods to live in sacred space. We were a social movement, lesbians creating women's land. The connections were so clear: loving women, loving the Earth. Living close to the Mother, learning from Her natural processes, tending Her body hands-on. We would go deep with Nature, with each other—inventing a new sub-culture away from the patriarchal mainstream. What would we become, what would we discover, creating our own world in the lap of the Goddess?

We did not discover utopia. Disappointments, conflicts, poverty, isolation, backlash pressured our fledgling communities, dwindled our numbers. Land-based living is hard work, and Mother Nature—for all Her generosity—is a rigorous teacher. She can insist, no matter what I have planned for a given day, that the long road be ditched during a pouring rain, that the long waterline be repaired after an animal's bite through. She is a tough lover. Her wasps sting, her bears sometimes claim the apples, her rabbits munch on vegetables, her snowfall downs trees. I bow to what I cannot control.

And, on the other hand of discovery, what an amazement it is to control so much. To be responsible for the water system that supplies my house, to make the fires that keep it warm, to have made the house—with the help of many women—in the first place. There is no Authority here, other than the mighty elemental powers, other than lesbian ingenuity.

Now and Then Mothering

I

Today I came upon a just-born butterfly.
Shy, startled to be outside her safe swirl of cocoon,
She clung tight to the grass stalk
Then let me be her mother.
After a few centuries,
I was thinking of teaching her to fly,
When there was a tiny whir of wings
And she was gone.
Mother-love: Quick to wonder   Eager to possess
Nervous about flight instruction.

II

Today I nursed a butterfly to health.
It had almost drowned in the orange juice can where
        marijuana seeds were soaking.
The mystery is too thick for me to know
If she was yesterday's butterfly,
But I know that she was my precious child
And I was fierce for her life—
Mary and Demeter and Isis and all grieving mothers
Stirring my hot patience,
Sending sunshine and warm breezes.
Come, little one,   Can you use this foot?
Standing up finally, a flutter of wet nowandthen wings,
Perched on my finger—all luminous orange and fur—
What do you do with a pet butterfly?
I put her on the tree stump altar
Where she sucked daisies long and hard
Her proboscis slender and strong.

Sunday, I went back to the altar and
Draped a snake carcass   Around the poison oak bush.
Mother Birth   Mother Death
Holy   Holy   Holy

The Lion and The Goose: Eclipse

Puma. Puma came last night
and made off with The Goose
offed The Goose
>   Precious Moon Goose
>   big gray bird
>   how intelligent your eye was
>   how interesting your conversations
>   screeches and honks, clucks and tut tut tuts
>   how sweet you were in the springtime,
>   coming round to say "Pet me please"
>   letting me stroke your elegant arch of neck
>   following me pad pad pad waddle waddle

pad pad pad Puma's paws in the night
right up to the house   right up to Moon Goose

We heard her cry out
"Help!" she said. "Come quick, something awful is happening!"
We ran out the back door, Yelling
"You can't have my goose!"
"Let go of that goose!"
>   Moon Goose, I heard your death
>   heard your bones crunch
>   heard your beautiful neck break.
>   There, it's over now.   It doesn't hurt any more.
>   I love you Moon Goose.
I did not see you
but racing down the back stairs,
I saw a lion
mountain lion down on the ground.
Giant Cat. Huge, a Zoo Cat.

"OH!"
We stop, change course
Up the stairs, I run for brighter light
but Puma pad pad pads away
into the brush. Crackle!   Like bones.

Puma snapped you up, Moon Goose.
Snap. It was a snap
for a lion to haul off a goose.

    A big gray goose
    sleeping on her rock outside the hen house door
    soft innocent downy feathers left behind
    a handful—that's all the goose there is.
    Tomorrow we will pad into the brush aways,
    Did Puma leave more of you around?
    Did the thick quills stick in her throat?
    Strong ribs of feather that would flap
    flap flap flap you off the ground sometimes
    you would soar toward the sky
    And glide
    gentle
    to ground.
    Sometimes you would hide exquisite works of egg
    among downy feathers, a nest of plucked self.
    You were bossy, fierce with your chicken friends,
    hostile to the collie, once to me.
    A Moon Goose of many phases.

Swamp bird, at home on the flat Nile
Webbing your way on this rough hillside.
The Nile Goose, they say, is Mother of All.
Great Chatterer, hatching the Sun itself
from downy feathered cosmic egg.

Puma.   Cougar.   Leo.
Beast of the Sun.
She pulls the brilliant chariot,
Flanks Lilith,
Carries Tara, plays with Circe and Artemis.
Sekmet, Fire-Lion.
Bast, Cat Who Destroys.
The Sun Beast comes golden and quick.
She devours the Moon
Goose Goose Goose Goose Goose Goose Goose.

Small Wonder

The roar of hummingbird wings—six pair of them
whirring buzzing harassing each other
around their 4-seater plastic syrup flower.
They dart in to feed, one at a time,
flare tiny fans of tail at each other
square off in mid-air
then dive bomb at ferocious speed
little feather bullets
red necks glisten, green wings shine
furious morsels of beauty,
clicking and clattering   *Get out of here! Go away!*
clicking and clattering scarcity belief, territorial war.

I swear it to you:
The moment of miracle happened
this very evening   sudden truce.
Six small sudden birds
sit down to eat together
gather around their dining table
four on the chairs, two hover close then share a plate
It was a blessed time.
Grace, in the hummingbird world.

Grace to my clicked and clattered heart,
heartweary of homefront battle.
I did not know that I was praying.
But my desperate need to see family gathered,
to feel the joy of shared homing—
must have breathed a powerful prayer.
And the hummingbirds,   all six cherubim,
imaged me answer,   image extraordinary hope—still
that the usual patterns of attack and defend
can drop away in a flash of bright wing
in a soft flurry of forgiveness
in a concerted hum of peace.

Witness

A bright morning
A steady pace down the forested road
Bridget and MahLi gallumph and sniff
and trot their doggy way
    stop to listen
I stop to listen
A rhythmic rasping whir
up ahead, to the right
"OK, dogs, let's turn around soon"
The neighbor man
is running some machine
    turning the woods into straight-up conifer columns
    taking out the curvy madrones
    the flowering manzanitas
    that graced the once unmanned drive into women's land
    roadside stark now with tree bodies and brushy debris
Ouch, it hurts to see this
even if I buy some of the madrone for my own woodstove
take my own chainsaw to the piled branches he leaves

But wait:
The rhythmic rasping whir—
    not a machine at all
    high up in a sinuous tree
The biggest bird I ever saw
Flapping giant dark wings
Rhythmic rasping   *What in the world?* Eagle?
"MahLi, come. MahLi, MahLi . . ."
The little one, blond fluff of dog
talon-sized morsel she is
running fearless toward the mystery
which, suddenly, is still, quiet, invisible
somehow merged with the tree
no bird at all
where once birdzilla was beating the air.

"MahLi, come!"

Then, unfolding from the tree
lifting into sky and off to the west
the languid, graceful stretch—ah yes! of Vulture.
Long elbowed span tipped with feather fingers
No interest in a lively Shi Tzu.
"It's OK, MahLi!"
Relief smiles in my chest.
My eyes pass by the tree—and freeze, disbelieving:

Turkey Vulture sits on a big, high branch
fluffed out black with her strange red head
Turkey Vulture Number Two!

And I am laughing loud.
Rhythmic whir, indeed.
Enormous flapping wings, the flap of more than one bird
Quite a flap they had made
Turkey Vultures fucking high up in a tree
Where else would they do it?
Why not?

And why not, goddess, let me witness
on a bright morning
    when some curvaceous trees lie dead
    their flesh ripe for human plucking,
    why should the dark carrion-angels
    not also make life   make wonder
    on an ordinary,
    extraordinary forest morning?
No bird more holy than this: Mut, Isis, Nekhbet
Mother Life   Mother Death   Mother Vulture
She who devours what she brings forth
All vultures are female, the ancients say

So: High in a sensuous tree
She loves up her sister
Sister Vulture
Sister Tree.

Snow, and White Noise

White is Hushed
White is Still
White is a cathedral
Thick silence over the land
A soundless carpet
White lays her quiet hands on the earth,
Movement stops.
A small bird flies down the aisle
Bushes are kneeling
Some trees are bowed
Others stand tall, shoulders draped with heavy robes—
A mute choir, lifting glorious songs of unspoken eloquence.

Listen. There is nothing to be heard.
If you listen carefully, you can hear Nothing.
White has so softened all sound
      that Nothing has become audible.
White has frozen all ordinary voices.
White ushers me in.
I stop. My ears breathe deeply.
Sometimes I listen to the Nothing.
Sometimes I fling a glorious anthem of my own
      toward the gray arches of sky,
Dare to break the veil of quiet with a yell
That drifts over the cushioned hills
And falls thoroughly into the plush mounded blanket—
No echo now from vaulted ridges
One loud prayer at a time
One white whisper.

On the high wire of these times
Changing Woman dances
surefooted and exuberant.
O Goddess of Radical Alchemy!
Teach us the arts
Of bending with the sway,
Then countering the flow,
Of blending the extremes,
Daring to hold the Middle Way.
Grant us, Kwan Yin,
Your poise in the eye of the storm.
Ground us in your Harmony.
Challenge us with the immeasurable reach
Of your Love.
Pele, Divine Artisan, temper us
In your Great Fire of reconciliation
Where opposites burst into new gold,
Rigidities soften
And the annealed heart can mend.

Invocation for We'Moon 2014: Radical Balance

SisterLove

Passion and Compassion © *Francene Hart 2003*

Temple Poem

It is not just that I love one woman
Invite her into the hushed temple of my most sacred self
Travel with her into the far corners
of her most private being.

It is not just that I am coupled:
I have coupled with her, and with her, and with her.
I am tripled, and quadrupled.
I am a throng of worshippers
reverent before our own images
jubilant to invent our own litanies.

I, quietly, by the thousands,
have stepped into a shrine of my own making.
I, and the multitudes of women who have slipped
silently away from the man's ceremonies.

Quickly!   Here is the path—
They never imagine that we have dared to come
right into the heartbeat of Love
naming it Woman,   calling it Holy.
They never suspect that we will decorate the altar with mirrors
dance praise to breast and womb   as it was in the beginning.

As it is now,   the tabernacle is invisible
and they cannot read our codes.
Sister pilgrims file into the circle,
we speak in tongues of song and drum
Shhh!   Do not chant the mysteries outside!
Blasphemy: this love of ourselves
Heresy: this adoring.

I have peered behind the inmost veil
and discovered a myriad of me—
I, and all these tribeswomen, charmed with power to fire galaxies
mapping new ventures of soul
spell-bound to each other and to the earth
as it evermore shall be.

Fly Away Home Ritual

I

Silence

The women are silent.
All day. Both of them.
Most every day.
Until supper, when they sing a song
      and eat a meal
      and rave about the food they grow
      report on dreams, dog and cat events of the day,
          the newest aching joint
          the latest flower-bed scheme.

Keepers of the quiet forest temple.
Keepers of quiet: a magic trick of tongue and will
      to make Solitude
      in the company of another.
Each one free to hear the plants grow and die
to follow the deep sound of private mind.

Keepers of temple: and women come
only women come
to be still
to sing out their hearts
to wear the spirits
in between one world
and another.

II

Hallowmas

The women are silent:
All day. They arrive by noon
and sit in circle together, many silent women.
Their minds are stilled. They breathe the quiet.

20

One by one, they stir, attend to food or walk or touch,
climb forested paths, visit the garden.
Silent. Listening
to the barest flutter of wing,
the rarest chortle of frog,
hen chatter.
Tuned to the whispers of earth
the shy messages of soul.

The day moves,   silent.
Faces speak friendship beyond words.
Women stroll the round house.
Slowly, slyly, they drape themselves with color
fabrics and paints
softly hover at the mirrors
smile to see each other disappear
into the space between the worlds.

Hallowmas

Feathers and bones, glitter and wigs
Hat, masks, robes:

> Whom do you invoke?
> With what spirit do you clothe yourself?

We open the costume trunk wide
It is the space between the worlds.

Late afternoon. The spirits and the women
sit in circle together
Silent, until the first of them shakes the rattle,
        shakes out her song
            sings   her heart open to the New Year
and the circle throbs, whoops, hums
tendering each song,
each singing healing woman
each visiting spirit
world upon world.

Homing
A Poem for Nome

I can feel her heart beat
soft thuds in a fragile cage of feathers and bone
My hands cup her tenderly
Her feathers are snow white, her eye rabbit pink
and she is eager to be loose.

They are all eager
They flutter and coo in our hands—
all twentysome of them.
We stand in Circle
we women, we birds, we women holding birds—
twentysome of us.
We watch the woman
who lifts each handful of bird
        from the bursting box of them
watch her skillful fingers wrap
        around flight-hungry wings.
She smiles at the next birdless woman,
speaks gently, "Here, like this"
and presses pulsing fluff into nervous palms.

She is shy to be priestess, but sure of her gift,
brilliant in her offering of these exotic moments.
We watch for her signal.
There: she chooses the moment.
She lifts her birdful hands toward the sky
We all lift birds and hands
a slight toss
and let
go

A skyful of white wings!
Quick! They are so quick to circle and soar
They are one creature now
one circle of freedom sailing around
our lifted heads
and away . . . disappearing . . .
gone.

But no, the high white circle returns,
wings around us again, again wings away.
They are loose,
and they are homeward bound.
They will be waiting for their woman
when she returns to her home.

She will smile and coo with them
She will feed her many creature-friends
those who feather, those who fur.

She is a homing woman.

Her creatures bark and purr and caw—
and cup the fragile cage of her life.
She is eager for their wisdom.
She watches.
She practices flying.
Her wings grow strong,
and brave.

For Susan
Disappearing Her Breast Lump

I am diving toward the fathoms of you
with my talons sharp to puncture the distance between us
to scratch the message of my loving,
fierce urgent scribble on the bare rock of emergency.
Not a soft feather nestle,
my loving for you has not been to cradle,
my loving for you has been to applaud.

> Respect thunders
> you dazzle my sky
> your art strikes genius
> I flash envy
> then I use you for light.

> See how small my ambition garden grew back then,
> before you rained challenge on me
> before your praise got me fertile,
> your example set me to bud.

I have flowered past daily terror now.
Sloth remains: you would spot it right away.
I do not so often play with spooks.
But I still think thoughts like "Weather is God."
It is raining. I am writing you
plunging into the crevice terror made,
chasing into the wake of alarm
to shout my love,   my faith
that you are taut and pure with power.

Your danger spurs me sudden, swollen
with feeling I am dashing to you.
Block me if you must,
but let my winging love flutter close
to tumble you a poem
to toss you a wordflower.

Beth at 50

I share name with you.
Beth—in Hebrew, "House."
And the syllable is holy
in words like Beth-El, House of God
Elizabeth, Consecrated to God.
I do not share altar with you,
rarely do we ritual together
but there is priestess work you take into the wide world
and I give you honor for the prayer your life is:
    Invocation for Justice.
Your life, this prayer, is not meek
It does not mumble in the corner
It dares—vigorous, clear—
in meeting rooms where the holy syllables
    Lesbian
have never before been spoken
It makes demand
in creative ways that reach to the heart of the people.

    There is a name for this one,
    She who channels the fire of righteous fury
    and stokes it at the public crossroads:
    She is Prophet.

I thank you, Beth, for being prophet among us.
I thank you for being angel on-the-job.
The science of your skill
    touching broken bodies with hope,
    professional in the business of mercy,
    repair, possibility
    your work a gift to children
    a labor of faith
It must be laced sometimes with despair
It must be sprinkled with wonder.

Your prophet, your angel
surely must rant and rave
and grieve from time to time
when Obstacle seems larger than Transformation
but what I know of your witch
is that she works the powerful magic of wit:
    she brews spicy stews of laughter
    quick and clever tidbits of irony or pun
    juxtaposed concepts that just might
    tickle the rib of a closeted bigot
    sparkle the smile of a damaged child
    guffaw a roomful of lesbian friends.

I thank you for the witch you are.
Your cauldron is a big heart.
You house compassion and fun,
and the Beth you are
is valuable architecture
in the landscape of community
I call home.

For Hawk Madrone at 70

Dogs know.
Dogs look into the smiling eyes   feel the soul embrace
of this woman who has been loving them   for lifetimes.

Any dog.
Dog in the back of a truck at BiMart
Dog in the park   Dog by the side of the road
Dog at the Shelter
The Shelter dogs are the ones most awestruck
   by this angel who gives them touch and walk
   and comfort, of an afternoon.

I know.
I have been watching this woman for 35 years.
The sights I have seen!

I watched as she and I held the snake
   and she ever so carefully cut away the tangled bird netting,
   scissors slipping precisely under the tight plastic cords,
   tight against soft scaly unscathed skin.

I have stood holding the fence post as she pounded,
   heavy sledge rushing inches from my head—
   knowing she would never miss.

I watched her build finely crafted cabinets, doors, windows,
   drawers, stairs, shelves,
   gates   and more gates   and yet another gate.

I have seen her transform a brushy hillside,
   choked with honeysuckle, blackberry, poison oak,
   into a lush cascade of flower beds—
   decades she has done this work,
   still she expands the tended reach,
   digs up, improves, amends, moves plants, adds new ones.
   Her face lights with wonder in a flower's glow.

I have seen her, countless times, on her back
   under the rusty truck, face flecked with truck debris,
   using this tool, now that, to insist a bolt *will* budge.

She does insist.
Her bark is worse than her bite.   I know.
This is a tender-hearted cur-mudgeon.
She is more shy than you know.

I have heard her sobs, all the way up the hill,
    when she found the little wren mama
    dangling dead from its nest.

I have been witness to this woman's grief—
    love gone missing. She gave her heartbreak to
    the dogs, the trustworthy ones.

Soft.
I remember that her feet are especially soft,
    and so the iconic story in my ancient heart-shrine
    is of a day, 35 years ago—we were high on mushrooms
    and romance—this woman walked all the way up Flagg Mountain
    in her bare feet. In her bare, tender feet.

I will walk with this woman, I said to myself.
And I have, I do, on this mountain, round and about
    our different paths, our common ones.

I have watched her change, grow,
    retool herself to the delicate technologies of computer, camera
    (old dog learning new tricks)
She has perfected the arts of solitude
    books read, pies baked, prose penned
    hands and imagination busy, accomplishing—
    a mastery of self-care.

She walks Flagg Mountain barefoot every day,
    you know—perhaps you don't know—
    an inner world of high-pitched sounds
    scream non-stop in her head.
    She is brave to be alive, I say.
And she gives of herself
    shares this forest refuge with women who come for its solace
    offers   wisdom to those who seek her counsel

footrubs at the ready
    exquisite writerly critique   exquisite writing
    a regular, frequent letter to an old, old woman
        still in the nursing home where her mother aged and died
    carpentry skills to help friends building
    companionship to help a friend dying

She has figured out, even, how to navigate
    the narrow, squabble-pocked streambed of
    unarticulated love between us:
    the gift of a mended chair
    thrift-store pants that always fit me
    advice and support for the overwhelming project
    hands-on when my bolt won't budge
    praise for my own word-craft.

She steadies my ladder.   I steady hers.

Two golden dogs race along the lane,
rough and tumble their play.
They give this woman daily laughter,
keen hearing, deep brown devoted eyes.
She adores them back, cooks them vats of healthy stew,
rubs their every inch with her fingers.
Knobby fingers now: I have been watching.

I went looking for Dog Goddesses.
    Ninkharak: Mesopotamia   Nehalennia: Celtic
    Dog Goddesses of Healing and Protection
Yes!   This is who she is,
This is who she runs with.

May there be packs of them—
    all manner of fluffy and scruffy and sleek,
    tails wagging wildly
when she gets to the Great Evermore
where D-O-G is G-O-D
and Muphin, her most beloved, is waiting.

For Sarah at 60

I

The Leonine Sun shines
from the bright star
of stage, of classroom, of home as art.
Oh, she would resist the accolades
insist that she missed the boat of grandeur
that she tames vocation-lust into a medium sparkle
quietly burnished with satisfaction
when students flame into understanding
and colleagues notice.

But when she belts it out
    in a gospel song
    a full throat prayer to Night Sky Goddess
    an exquisite lilt of body and voice
        shaping a character just so
    an elegantly timed slice of wit
        right in the midst of everyday talk
there are not enough bushels to hide this light
this luminous Power
Power of Sarah.
Let it rip!

II

Your birthdate shimmers in my world.
Before I knew you, I would already stop and honor this day.
August 6 brought my mother into life
    1922
A fiercely radiant star
50 years she blazed
and I swung round in grateful orbit
At least that is one way to slice the myth.
I say her name: Rebecca
Your name: Sarah
Sarah and Rebecca

The mythic trap doors fall open
and I am in Genesis with Abraham and Isaac
and Jacob and Esau, Hagar and Ishmael, Rachel and Leah
Sarah and Rebecca. Cousins and in-laws.
Family woven tight, woven tribal
these ancient peoples splicing, stitching layers of kinship.

There is a layer of sister between us
Not the way friend seeks out friend
More the way sisters wind up in the same weave
threaded together in this triangular tapestry
You bound to her, I bound to her
therefore you and I bound together.
And how marvelous to find you wonderful
        to rejoice in your presence
        and seek your friendship gladly.

III

I must speak, also and alas,
of the people who died on August 6.
140,000 of them
        1945
Hiroshima
I stop, and honor this day.
The trap doors of horror fell open
Empire of the Rising Sun blazed unspeakable
Atrocity on a day of precious births
Precious these dead ones
sacrificed at the altar of War
where the fabric of humankind
        lies forever in tatters and shreds.

"You shall save alive nothing that breathes,
you shall utterly destroy them, the Hittites and the Amorites,
as the Lord God has commanded."

Nonsense, He did no such thing . . . What Lord God?

The sisters, the mothers know
of the deeper cord that holds us
They slip into the War temple
    gather up the scattered thread and crumbs of cloth
    set up their needles and looms
    under cover of Night Sky Goddess
    they weep their tears into beads
    they spin smiles of love into fresh yarn
    weaving, mending the sacred circle
Sacred sisters   Weave and mend.

IV

I sing sistersong to you.
I sing decades of summer visits
when you sling firewood and build salads
and restore your soul, in the lap of the Mother
on the arm of your true sister.

And I, without woman sibling of my own,
        get woven in.
The shower of Holiday gifts comes to me as well—
you know how to do this family thing
And the Kinship Goddess knows how to distribute her gifts,
no random threads in this design—
I look at you: Theaterwoman
You look at me: Theaterwoman
We could not have staged it more perfectly.

Nothing   more perfect than when we—you and she and I—
blend bright harmonies
    I can lean into melody or trip into parallel tones and you
    are always inventing some vibrant steady trill, always
    soaring us toward some Pleiades
    where
Sure as the wind, you are my sister.

You turn 60.
And I am happy to sing you this
Sarahsong.

The Butterfly Effect

I am studying the science of Chaos—
the new mind-games in which physicists
and mathematicians once again are discovering
The Goddess.

They amuse themselves, saying
mayhaps a butterfly stirring the air in Beijing
can transform storm systems next month in New York.

The universe whirs with random events
unpredictable patterns—tiny, odd changes
which create, in the aggregate, massive discontinuity.
Disorder, which displayed beyond imagination
on bright computer screens,
nonetheless graphs out into shapes of elaborate beauty
Goddess fingers fibered with exquisite geometric structure
lavish spirals of color and form:
the mark of Grand Design
seen close up, or from very far away—
Wildness, divine artist, at intricate play.

I am studying the Chaos in my recent love with you
the breakdown in the romantic system between us
There is no distinct butterfly to be found
but we were caught in a storm of discontinuous events
tiny, odd occurrences which fascinate my pattern-play
and strike me with elaborate hindsight beauty:
material and psychic realms oddly swirled together
in a dynamic of surprise that was, in the aggregate,
close up, and now from very far away,
about our separation
and nothing was random after all.

Take, for example, erratic behavior
of letters, our last two weeks,

caught in the predictable Post Office
unpredictable delay after delay
pieces of love gone awry,
truth oscillating.

Take, the fancy typewriter I gave you at Solstice
bundled with you from airplane to airplane,
stolen your first night home,
the neat linear equation of gift, one to another,
fractured—radical intervention of unknown function.

Take, two flat tires, one after another,
on the day you drove to me at the airport,
our last visit.
You drove with news of your love gone awry
stirred and transformed with another woman
your passion for me deflated.
A swarm of butterflies punctured your dutiful momentum
the pressure of change
of desire at zero velocity.

Take, a day in late December.
Your first touch with your new flame.
Four days out of my arms, you begin new loving.
A butterfly stirs the air.
1500 miles away, I savor my passion for you
        a quiet afternoon storm of sure feelings
        overcoming random jealous fear
        of some Eventual day you would begin new loving.
There is no provision in the general theory of relativity
for instantaneous transmission of energy
at any speed greater than the speed of light.
        So it must have been with the speed of light
        that my body registered discontinuity
        and I reached up in the dim evening
        to light an oil lamp,

did not see the lamp already bright
the glass chimney was hot
and it burned my thumb and my fingers
with a wild and sudden heat
wild and sudden, like your heat 1500 miles away.
The graph of that day must be a flower
on someone's computer screen,
a jewel of spittle on the Goddess's chin
as She throws her head back to laugh
at perfect eruptions of disorder.

Perfect, we used to say,
folded up close as butterfly wings
at rest in the wonder of loving,
synchronous events clustered sweetly around us
in tidy geometries of Magic.

Wild, we used to say
of our intricate flying play,
flesh and mind.
Wild, I say now, from very far away
where I can see that the Grand Design
is not only pretty,
it swings as well into jagged occurrence
rips at the heart with a day's stormy news
burns fingers with space-time fluctuation.
There is no smooth curve to trace on this chart:

There are the wildly gesticulating arms of
a random, dervish Goddess who tosses me about,
and my work, my gift
is to fathom that the sum of this chaotic tossing
actually lands me in some new cocoon
where elaborate glory is just bursting to be born
and some new wild pattern
is flexing gossamer possibility.

The Fairy Godsisters Scene
from *Feathers in My Mind*

[Cinderella, Bethroot's fairy tale persona, wears a crown of golden fabric, and has been puzzling about romance and marriage with three magical characters in fanciful masks: Fairy Godsisters, drawn from Bethroot's once-upon-a-time lesbian family circa 1980.]

CINDERELLA

Maybe *you* have it figured out: marriage and romance and commitment and family.

SISTER DELIGHT

Some days I want to eat numbers, be a color, dive into a molecule, walk an unknown planet, tame a wild beast—and I do not want you there. You or you or you. Any of you. Some days I want to do it all alone, all by myself. The thrill, the exquisite terror, the unshakable peace of me myself. Solitude is my whet-stone. I use it to sharpen the blade of my self. I cut clean, free of attachment.

[*Chuckling*] But my passion with you, my sister, is strong and easy. I can be a glutton. I could sit at the feast table all day long. I could make love to you morning and night. I run my hand to where the curls are thick and dark and moist, the mushroom gills of you slippery with desire. I love hearing you gasp and croon with joy, I catch my breath, we flick the tips of our tongues together, hard, a struggle of tongues, my clitoris buzzes breathless.

My loving is over all the skin of you. And the look of an angel is on your face. I tender you, you baby me. This is sweet, pure pleasuring innocent and juicy, delicious with genuine liking, minds winking joy off and on through the day.

SISTER WISDOM

I created this womanhomeland with my sister, and it is holy. Our struggles are sometimes awesome. We fill the valleys with our pain. The green trees, the night animals absorb our cries. When there is nothing left to believe in, I believe in the green trees, the animals, the certainty of moonrise,

Our love is fierce and holy. We have lived through hatred. We exiled one another, we no longer share erotic sacrament. We continue to create miracles. We have prayed for women to come and circle and enfamily with us, and they do. We are learning daily grace. We share old stories and creature-love and hearth-tending.

I will go with you, my sister, into the emergency rooms, into the silent halls of your loneliest nightmare. I may not be the one who draws closest to your heartbeat. But I will tend you. I will sit for long hours at your bedside and hold your aged hand. You can count on me until the end. Bedrock love, layered with faults. Commitment that depends not on this year's feeling or that, but on purity of will, devotion to an extra-ordinary dream of green trees and certainty.

SISTER MUSIC

My sister and I play in the fresh fields of imagination together. Making up the stories, taking the risks—hurling ourselves out there in front of 200 eyes: it is orgasm high, it is a cold shower for the mind. JUMP! and I am on the hot griddle, sizzling with power, vibrating, as much in her hands, she as much in mine, as though we were making love.

We gather our playmates and open the magic boxes, waving colors, casting spells. Invention is always the challenge; the games—inexhaustible. My sister and I are brilliant to create around us women who want to play. Every night we play dinner. We play farm, and we play ritual. A family of friends, of choirgirls come home.

And when my sister sings with me the soft rich croon of a lullaby, I am listening to the voice of all mothers, a blanket of sound, tucking the eternal child into warmth. We have been mothers, and sisters before: in the corridors of forever, where twins spiral in and out of lifetimes, and Color and Sound make up play after play.

CINDERELLA
      Oh, I want to be in *your* fairy tale! I want to be alone and in love and committed and surrounded by compassionate friends. I wish I could be a Fairy Godsister with you all.

[*Cinderella removes her crown, and, with a flourish, happily takes up a mask of her own as Sister Harmony.*]

SISTER HARMONY
      I am marrying my girlfriends.
      We have gone far deep together,
      trusted each other in the most intimate
                  circumstances.
      I live in plenty of opportunity for feeling
      my heart open wide, the facets of me reflected
      as my sister or my sister or my sister walks by.

[*Sister Harmony becomes Bethroot*]
BETHROOT

In the Year 2030:
Ancient winged reptile
old turtle, scales and wrinkles—still I fly
millions of years in these cells
a feathered soul, in the sky of time.

Our faces have been so much fun—these past decades,
watching the crust fold in
watching the soft river of age
estuaries of line, deltas spread on floodplains
where the gestures of our skin tell who we are.

We wear our stories in plain sight.
I greet you with my self-portrait,
and we are especially amused at the new information we plot
autobiographies of smile and frown
deeper disclosure every year.

Loving you, this half-century
Loving the women I love, this half-century
I have learned body and beyond.
Auras mingled deep, we have learned the senile secrets:

Take Beauty.
These past decades, and still
green fire dances in your eyes
your beauty is child-bright
and there is no mistaking you
in old lady disguise.

Take Death.
These past decades, and still
dreams dance you into my heart
your being is life-bright
and there is no mistaking the feathers
you drop into my mind.

Shapeshifter!   Magician of the Night.
Now we see you—Now we don't
Now we see you again
How astonished we were,
deep in the original eon
when humanity was a babe
and we first saw the darkness
gobble you up
then saw you grow back—
over and over.
How can this be?
We bow down with awe,
reach to you in wonder.
Jezanna, Ixchel, Hina, Menos
We call you by innumerable names
Selene, Anahita, Neith, Mama Quilla
We worship you with terror and praise
Mother of Life and Death
Mother of Time
We scratch days on our calendar bones . . .
Lo! We bleed—just so—
as you dance   you mirror
Steady is your rhythm
Magnet Mother
You pull our blood, you pull the Great Waters
capillaries and pools, eddies and plasma.
Dreams and hunches. Madness. Illusion.
Changing Woman
you hold, you yield   flood and recede
befriend darkness, unveil soft light.
Born to walk your Moonwise path,
we trust
Your Revolution.
Blessed Be.

Invocation for We'Moon 2018: La Luna

Sacred Roots

Prayer © Toni Truesdale 2014

Suddenly I Am Demeter

Suddenly I am Demeter.
Fifty-two years I have been daughtering,
the myth turned upside down:
my mother dead, two decades.
I was Perserphone grieving,
Demeter lost in the nether world.

But now another twist of myth,
and I am full of motherly heart,
lighting candles for the maiden
who frolics in a dangerous world.

My brother's child, grown woman now,
is newly birthed into my life
as though she sprang full blown from someone's forehead
as though she rose full foamed from the cresting sea.

She came to visit the temple
came to inquire of the priestess.
She brought her eager mind
her radiant spirit
her troubled past
yearnings to shape a new future.

We played together for days
pouring stories, spilling secrets,
mining family lore.
We laughed and cried
unfurled sacred scrolls
entertained oracular games
watched shooting stars
discussed the suffering planet.

The temple choir sang perfect harmonies
The young woman's face lit with wonder
and depth of understanding.
I had seen those same shining eyes
in her baby days
I had seen that same chiseled beauty
in my young mother.

A new chapter opens in my life
New and precious friendship
kinship going deep
kinswoman taking her place in my close circle.

And she is off
into the pathways of her very different life
into the raunchy bars, the violent risks of an urban Hades.
She carries a smolder of temple flame
to show herself new steps.

I light candles, speak her name.
I call to her:
Remember the soft singing strength.
Be nourished by your holiness.
Stay away from pomegranates.

*In the Greek myth that overlays earlier matriarchal strata,
Persephone happened to bite into a pomegranate just before her
release from captivity in Hades, violating the rule that she not eat
anything in the underworld, and consigning herself to Hades for
one-half of every year. The pomegranate had long been associated
with Goddess worship in the Ancient Near East; the Greek story
transforms it into a dangerous fruit. The poem uses this later meaning.*

Miracle in Two Parts

I

The family was accustomed to miracles.
"The Lord will provide!"
Granddad insited that Sunday evening
as he set out to find food   penniless
the preacherman and his family
arriving at the new parish house too soon
before the country congregation had time
to pay them with ham and roast chicken, dumplings, cherry pie.

He gathered them round the piano to pray and sing
The hymns would ripple with Grandmother Moms' skillful chords
And her golden contralto, his charcoal baritone
would shimmer and ring the certainty of grace
      never mind the empty larder.
The children must have been old enough to blend with skill
Mama's clear soprano, Uncle Tom the young tenor
Uncle Robert with child-voice sweet and full, deepening already.
They were a heavenly choir
      opening hearts and moistening eyes
      in revival tents and country churches
      on the circuits of the Cumberland Presbyterian fold.
They were singing for their supper this Sunday night
in yet another manse to be home for awhile.

"The Lord will provide," Granddad promised
"You just keep singing!"
And they did, while he walked out the door
and down the road to forage in the vineyard of his Lord.
The story is told, and he must have told it,
that he walked a fruitless path
the way was long, there was no supper at hand,
      when lo! he looked down at his feet
      and the Lord had turned up a rabbit.
I do not recall hearing whether the rabbit was alive or dead
      but it was supper

45

And the story is quite clear
that the preacher returned triumphant to his hungry choir
and a miracle meal was enjoyed by all.

II

I have been drawn toward those Cumberland hills
family events calling me to honor
a niece who graduates, another who marries.
But money has seemed scarce for this sentimental journey.

A surprise letter comes from Uncle Robert.
He and Uncle Tom the only choir members left alive.
He sends a savings bond, just now turned up.
Grandmother Moms bought it in my name for $25 in 1968.
She has been dead for 16 years
This bond has been hiding out
waiting for just the right moment to spring
and Moms must have given the signal, spirit touching matter
just when I was hungry for a family feast.
She insists on my trip with a flourish:
    At the bank the bond has become $252,
    and I will be winging my way
    shimmering with grandmotherly grace.
We share telephone laughter—my nieces, my brother and I
We are amazed, and we are not surprised,
accustomed to miracles in our heritage.

I am humbled to find myself among those tribes
who bow to vigorous Ancestors,
and I will sing with new wonder
when the women I choir with begin the Circle song:

> *Grandmother, I see you standing in my life*
> *You are sacred. You are sacred.*
> *You are sacred.*
> *And you are looking at me.*
> *I pray to you, pray to you*
> *You are sacred,*
> *And you are looking at me.*

46

Root Food

The skillet is hot
and the crisp nubbins are browning
as if they were crumbles of sausage.
The eggs slide yellow into the black pan,
scramble around with the nubbins
and I am so pleased to create this illusion of
sausage and eggs
on a rainy Sunday morning.
Falafel patties crumble and crisp and spice up
as hot as any red peppered Tennessee sausage.

Sunday night suppers, sometimes
Mama would make sausage and eggs.
Sometimes, and in the early years,
the sausage would come wrapped in white paper
frozen from our rented meat locker across town
or it would come out of home-canned jars.
Katy Perkins told a tale about meeting Mama
for the first time, so beautiful she was
in a sharkskin cloth suit at the bridge party,
but she had to leave early, had to get home
to can sausage.
  It might have been 1945.
  It would have been cold.
  It had to be bitter cold for killing hogs.
  Daddy would go to the farm where he grew up.
  He and the tenant family
  would do whatever bloodshed and gore are meant by
  killing hogs.
In town, at kitchen table,
Mama and my grandmother Gee would be forearms deep
in dish pans full of raw ground meat
flecked with red pepper.
There would be an inch of grease at the top of each
hot packed jar.

I believe that Mama really wanted to stay at the bridge party
laughing and witty with sophisticated friends.
She did not really want greasy forearms
with a kitchen-queen mother-in-law.
Mama used to tell a recurring dream:
    Daddy is bringing home unexpected guests, she races
    to the refrigerator to create sudden banquet, there is
    nothing there, nothing but lettuce.
    Gee appears.
    Gee creates an elegant feast
    from nothing but lettuce.

At least we lived in town.
Mama was glad not to be stuck off in the country
which is where, after all, she came from.
Generations of workworn women behind her
Dirtgrimed hands proud of potatoes, beans, turnips, sage
Aprons stiff with flour-dust,
ovens yawning biscuits, sugary pies, cornbread.

In Mama's belly, I was cooking
when first she shared kitchen and house with Gee
the young bride, the reigning mother-in-law.
It was summer when I was swelling
and I'll bet that Mama was swearing
at the kitchenful of farm food
to be shucked and diced and canned
swearing secretly at the fussy woman she assisted.

And when I swear so quickly at my farm chores
at mountains of task to be shredded and chopped
I wonder—for the first time,
with the smell of browning morsels in a cast iron skillet,
I wonder if my quick fury is a stifled echo
of a young bride's discontent,
baked into my molecules.

Mama may wonder, with her spirit vision,
what I am doing here
with rows to be planted and harvest buckets to be hauled.
But the irony, pungent for both her and me,
is how much we relish—
Mmm, mmh doesn't that taste good?
      The yum of just that perfect bite
      the creamy blend, the savory mouthful.
      She was as proud as any farmwife
      of her eggplant casserole with pimento cream sauce
      tomato and celery aspic
      vegetable soup simmered all day with a beef bone.
      Her rolls were as fluffy as Gee's
      and her dinner parties, elegant.

I brown mock sausage on a Sunday morning.
I feed only myself.
There are no other beings who suck from my breast
depend on my kitchen finesse.
The domestic trap did sparkle with joy, deeper than taste buds:
Mama loved her children,
we were her soul food.
But she never did sit down on a Sunday afternoon
and stir up a poem,
fry up short stories for which she left recipes,
brew with care the novel she imagined.

This Sunday, after breakfast, after poetry,
I scrub Jerusalem artichokes,
knobby
dark with mud
root food.
Three bulging sacksful.
I will give a bag of them to my friends.
And I will serve a plateful
of poem.

A Stitch In Time

Dusky rose velvet
How can I scissor this lush cloth?
Cut through, no going back
I call out to my dead mama
So serene she is, her portrait there on the piano

Mama, how did you do this, cut irrevocably
into brocade, fine silk, Irish wool, melon-colored taffeta
wedgewood blue velvet—lace and tulle and tweed
expensive fabrics laid out on the dining room table
scissors following along the edge
of flimsy paper patterns stippled with straight pins

I am awed by your daring
This moment of risk I face unveils your great courage
The brave, decisive act   no less existential
than felling a tree   or taking scalpel to living tissue

I bow to "womanly" craft:
the power of homespun art in my mother's skillful hands
I scorned needle and thread—domestic, tedious, boring
or maybe I shied from her expertise
It was all a mystery to me
I would stand still for the hemming
happily wear the results
never once ask how a dress was made anyway

Now, a delicate textile repair for my theater art.
Complicated. Scary.
I must hide frayed luster with fresh-cut patches of dusky rose.
Straight pins hold my rough pattern in place.
Soft velvet lies open   innocent   vulnerable

Mama, help me do this!
Snip. Snip.
The woman who can sew a fine seam
can do anything.

Mama, I Tell You
the Mountains Are Moving

Mama, I tell you the mountains are moving!

I see it with my own eyes:
the women are coming
the women are coming together
    out of the hospital beds
    off of the X-ray tables
the women are coming together
by tens, by hundreds
bald-headed women
one-breasted women
with bodies scarred and carved
fried, and pickled with poison to attack
the poison they breathed, they ate, their children sucked.

I see it with my own eyes:
these women are sitting together
by tens, by hundreds
they are shy, they are angry
they are smiling at one another
they are touching hands
they are talking talking talking their stories
they are holding each other sobbing
they are walking to the front of the room
where the big drums have been pounding
they are taking the sticks in hand
they are beating the drums
they are drumming pounding drumming
they are laughing fiercely to be living
they are living, and fierce, and together.

And Mama, the breasted mountains are shaking.

I knew, with my own vision,
when you lay broken and moaning
your chest flattened and stitched
brain, bone, lung on fire

I knew
    that someday the flaming women would erupt
    someday they would drum the bedrock into motion
    they would fault the poisonmakers,
    find each other with cadence of love and fury.

And how you would have loved to be among them, Mama
how gleefully you would have hurled yourself
into the quaking rhythm
you would be shouting laughter, woman to woman
you would be wild and comforted.

I close my brimming eyes.

I see you, Mama, and an army of your flat-chested ghost sisters
pounding pounding on the mantle of the world,
the drumskin is tight and thin,
the living women match you beat for beat—

no wonder the cliffs are trembling.

I need not tell you, Mama, that the mountains
are moving.

Mama Watching
from *Feathers in My Mind*

In the secret room of my self-definition
there is a mirrored cabinet
with mascara brushes
tiny bottles of perfume
berry-ripe lipsticks
magic making implements
from my enchanted days of Mama-watching.

In the secret room of my self-definition,
there is Mama.

You are inside me now.
I hear you in my voice, my idiom.
I see you in my mirror.

I remember you looking at me—
intense steady focus,
electric attention
a charged field between us.
I would feast my eyes on you,
magnetized by love, and judgment.

You are everywhere now.
I hear you in the endless certain sound of ocean
I see you in the fierce gray kitten
in the ripe green life of forests,
whenever the planet comforts me.

You pulse in my veins.
I flood with love for a woman in my arms
and you are rushing through me—
I am a conduit for eternal life.

Except when you are nowhere to be found:
a gaping tear in the fabric of sky
an empty wound, vacant, bloodless
the open scar of final loss
always fresh, always absurd.

Visitation

Tinkles, jingles
a tintinnabulation of mysterious,
delightful, maybe celestial ringing.
What IS that sound?
The laundromat door opens
A young Asian woman steps inside smiling
tinkling an array of glass wind chimes—
dozens of them—kitchy angels, hummingbirds, American flags
shimmering with sound.

She comes right to me
there at the folding table with my towels and shirts
a pedestrian day, an uneventful chore until now.

    "Hello. God bless you. My name is Mary Kim.
    I am a missionary from China.
    I am working with youth groups here to promote family values.
    Will you please support us with a donation?
    Here, have this lovely little bird, this chime."

    "Did you make these yourself?"
    "No, I did not make them. Here, take. . ."

    "I really don't agree with your program."
    "Thank you, God bless you."

    "But I could find a couple of dollars."
    I am won over by the smiling.
    "Thank you. God bless you. How many children do you have?"

    "No children."
    "No Children?!"

    "And I am not married—by choice."
    "Oh. God bless you. Thank you."

I come up with $3.
She bows her thanks, her blessing
and goes to a man folding sheets near the driers.

Always, she is smiling.
He turns his back to her and says "No."
The next man obviously lies, "I have no money."
"God bless you," she says to each one, bows her leave.

*   *   *

Some tide of history is in reverse flow
and takes me for a personal spin.
It is said that at my mother's birth, in 1922
her parents prayed aloud:
    "Thank you God! Our first little missionary to China!"
Missionaries to China—that was their dream.
It was my mother's childhood nightmare, recurring, over and over.
She would wake to terrified imaginings—forced to China,
where her parents would be eaten alive.
Prayers and prejudice notwithstanding,
there were no exotic mission fields in the family story.
Not until Granddad started ministering
on skid row in his old age.

Now the world is upside down.
An ordinary American laundromat
And we are the mission field.
We are the benighted society—rude, arrogant, privileged.
A young Chinese woman ministers with her blessing, her smiles.

Say it were a dream.
Say Mary Kim is some angel sent by my long-dead mother
    who loves ironies, and story
    sent to sparkle a tedious afternoon
    with cascading chimes, cross-cultural surprises,
    a warm heart, a family echo
    a geo-religious twist.

Say it all comes out in the timeless wash
    who blesses
    who is blessed
    who spins where at any given now
    in the Great Cycle.

Dear Goddess of Impenetrable Mystery—
Cerridwen, Hecate, Quilaztli, Kali—
What IS on The Other Side?
What is it like Over There?
Beyond the veil, across the abyss,
inside that other point of view,
among those other cultures,
in that creature's awareness,
after the revolution . . . .
You are the Certainty.
At the end of every life-path, you wait to harvest us,
to enfold us in The Great Transformation.
Help us to shed every old skin, every outworn pattern.
Reinvent us, Goddess of Beginning
Make us new, Goddess of The End.
Make us fit right through your needle's eye.
Stitch the new world with us.
Strange Mother,
Stay beside us
Give us courage for all our crossings.

Invocation for We'Moon 2013: The Other Side

She Comes For Us

Calling the Other Side © *Paula Franco 2010*

Saving Seeds

Curved lips of pod protect dry seeds from wet
until it is time for drench and sprout.
I walk in rain.
I curve my hands around the pod
they just fit, palm to palm,
a prayer to keep crisp safe from damp
they just fit—the pod itself now seed between my pod fingers

and I contemplate
Danger.
All the danger there is to protect from.
Grapes to protect from bird
strawberries to protect from raccoon
road to protect from deluge
water line to protect from freeze
firewood to protect from moisture
flowers to protect from deer
me to protect from cold, from drunk drivers,
icy steps, exotic bacteria

And I do not even live in a war zone
I do not live among poisonous snakes or on a flood plain
I do not live within two miles of human males
Human male: another way to spell danger,
for me, for planet.

So what if earthquake shakes my house down?
my beautifully crafted house
What if forest fire eats up my carefully arranged treasures,
my precise life-work.
So?   It is said: The teacup is already broken.
Ah. I see.
I can only hold onto the pod for so long.
I am a crisp and impermanent shield for the precious seed of myself
And I will split, as surely as
tectonic plates scrape past
as surely as planet falls into sun.

Ceremony for Nancy

Nancy loved white. Nancy loved blue.
I put on white pants, a fine white pullover
a ceremonial coat of many blue colors
    it belonged to Chris, also gone from this life.
I wear my transformation earrings
    the butterfly, the snake.
I place white mums in the Circle, at the South,
light the five white altar candles at Center.

A white poinsettia bears my name
in a church two thousand miles away,
where Nancy's friends gather in her honor.
I gather my holiness together in this, my temple my home,
and worship with them at the appointed hour.
Nancy's letters ring the Circle,
    strung together once with velvet ribbon
    for a theater piece on friendship.
Her wedding picture—soft maiden in white—is at my side.
I sound the brass singing bowl
tones echo round and round the lofty vault.
I have cleared the piano, dusted off the Methodist Hymnal.
I fancy them singing:
"Be Thou My Vision, O Lord of My Heart"
"For All the Saints, Who from Their Labors Rest"
I love to play these hymns, falter now,
    out of practice, out of sync.
More comfortably, in Circle I sing the Hers
    that belong to my present-day clan.

> *We All Come from the Goddess,*
> *and to Her we shall return*
> *Like a drop of rain,*
> *flowing to the ocean*

It is raining, and Nancy returns to Source.
I meditate. I cry.
I read aloud my "Nancy" poem, the one that tells our story.
I sing: "When They Ring the Golden Bells for You and Me"
    I ring a bracelet of golden bells
    I read my poem "Still Nancy," the story of our last visit, and
    how, at the end, she struggled free of brain tumor damage
    and spoke, clear as bells, her love for me:
"What's important   is to remember   I always   love you."
Then I Really Cry.
Thank you, Nancy. I always love you.

I tone—low, steady O, and harmonic notes play on top
    like angels singing.
I read three random letters from Nancy
    1964   1969   1974
I am absorbed.
I look up.
The sky is full of white!

It is snowing,
and Nancy returns to Source.
I always love you.
I tone—low, steady O, and the angels sing.
I sound the brass singing bowl,
tones echo round and round the lofty vault.

She Took Chris, Then Julie

Kali is on the prowl.
Watch out! She springs without warning
She has tasted fresh, young blood twice now among us.
Appetite whetted,
She was not content with one ambush
not sated with just one feast
on healthy, vibrant woman flesh.
She struck again, aimed deep into community heart.
      "Let me see," did She mutter through bloody fangs,
      "where is the next most robust morsel?"
Drunk, and hungry to eat promise again,
She sniffed the scent of joy
spit out the bitter suicide dregs of Her first kill
and, stealthy, silent, crept among us
skilled in the art of surprise
drawn to pulsing happy vigor.

Goddess, even in stupor, is perfectly lucid.
She took pity on us this time
let the last day of life be full of
      I love you, I love you, I am so happy
gave death with a veritable burst—we could say of joy
      pain was brief, end was quick
allowed us to touch and hold and carry
      the body of our cherished friend
      to watch irrevocable stillness
      the evolving purple, yellow, mottled bloom
      of cellular finish.

Not this one, we begged.
But Kali had made Her choice
Insisted that we feed her fiery maw
with this precious woman
who blazed into glory before our eyes.

We came from far and near, ached and cried,

rejoiced for the gift of this pure life.
There were no shortages of miracle:
hardened hearts among us softened
And then She Herself showed up at ceremony.

Goddess on Her belly   Snakewoman
    six feet long and swollen with Her meal
    gliding through green meadow grass toward our assembly
    creeping among us, underneath the circular platform
    bisecting the Circle—as is Her wont—to cut through.

Kali is not done with us.
Oh no, She has only begun.
The two skulls around Her neck are a starter set
She will be adding to Her necklace for years to come.
Old bones, wrinkled skin
satisfy her well enough, they are Her staple fare.
But She went out of order, broke into the clan and took our heirs.

This snatching of bright youth
    is aberration   is outrage
    is Her prerogative
And we are stunned by Her raw power
Her Absolute Mystery
Shall we say Holy Mother?
Can we say Blessed Be?

Ah, She is impeccable—this teacher of fierce lessons.
No holds are barred.   No one is safe.
The only promise is that we will, each one,
look into Her grinning face
Whenever She says
and be taken into Her Joy.
Her Holiness.
Her Strange Mothering.
Shall we say Mercy?
Shall we say Love?

Blessed Be.

Burial at Mountainlight

There is no sound
THUD
like the sound of fresh dirt
THUD
on the top of a coffin

There is no song
rising from my throat
in these stark moments

But there is no grave
like this grave
not for thousands of years

They dug for days
Sue and Sky   Melissa, Amara, Sequoia.
Four feet deep, seven feet long, three feet wide.
Amara and Sequoia and Sky
dug for more days, and when they had finished,
Amara, Sequoia, each one lay on the bottom
and understood the next step.
They returned next day
with buckets of white clay slip, and earth-orange plaster
They painted all day
paleolithic white walls, amber burnish
black earth designs—circles, spirals, swirls
rose gold berries and leaves shaping
signs of goddess/woman/dyke, signs of love and blessing engraved.
Beauty right there in the pit
Art on the smooth skinned belly
of the Mother—open to receive her daughter Silver.

We build our own houses   grow our own food
Why would we not bury our own dead?
We would burn them if we could, if they wished and law allowed
We would give them to the Vulture Goddess if it were permitted

There is at least this freedom
to dig into our Ground
    give each other to the Earth
    paint our emblems on the face of Death
    sing one another to rest.

The world is radiant with wonder this burial day.
Arrows of geese fly by, just in time for fly away songs.
Leaves cascade from branches when lyrics call for them.
A thick comforter of dark grey
clouds the wide sky, showers pummel distant ridges,
at any moment, downpour on our Circle.
Hours pass, perhaps four raindrops fall.

We sing and laugh, tell tales of our shining friend,
honor women for months of devoted care
tender bloodsisters far from home.
Prayer to Tara, Silver's special goddess.
Quiet.
A blue heron soars.

Then, drums beat steady.
Eight of us carry the box—she wanted a box—
down the field toward the big trees.
Miracle as we walk: sudden golden glow showers us
sudden sun goddess breaks from the clouds
Amataratsu—brilliant, in perfect time.
Our faces mirror Her smile.
She gives us moments, retreats again behind Her blanket.

The sacred task is smooth   tricky but smooth
ropes, timbers, women
lowering
wooden
casket
down
into
deep
cradle,

lined with women's love
resplendent with lesbian artistry
ancient magic reborn into this century
this Circle of Spirit-Revolution

Prayers and songs do come
sweetness and tears
It takes many songs, many shovels.
handsful of dirt
shovelsful
THUD. THUD. THUD.

The work is steady. I rest from singing.
And in the lull, an eerie, distant sound, like bagpipes.
Bagpipes!
A solitary, unseen friend offers her gift.
Amazing Grace: she plays for Silver.
We shiver with the fun of one more surprise.

At last the dark soil is piled.
It is enough.
Heart-stones are tenderly placed.
The Circle draws close, sings sisterly songs
We bless and are blessed.
We finish.
But it is not enough:
Goddess has more wonder to speak
Coyotes howl Her tune
precisely as clouds break open again
and a plump crescent moon
smiles Her grace.
Amazing.
There is no Silver lining
like this one.

Now: After Tee's Memorial

Now
there is an edge
when one of us asks another
How Are You?
The look penetrates.
Inquiry searching molecules, investigating spirit
peering past the curtain
to wonder Really
how you are.

Do you have cancer?   How's your heart?
Will you be next?

I scry into my own eyes
asking the mirrored woman
How will it come?   How long do I have?
Will I be ready?

No longer an idle question
How are you?

One by one
we are leaving this life
falling, one by one, like bowling pins
and we left standing for now
are knocked each time
even though we have always known the score.
Each new hit shocks to the marrow.
Nothing—not age, not fairness—
guarantees our place in line.

This friendship tribe of women
who make culture   make revolution
make deep with one another
holding on as long as we can

Now, it is easier to say
I love you.
Now, it is necessary.

Legacy'd
for Beverly Brown

Will you really, finally die
after I use all the Sweetmeat squash seeds
you gave us years ago? Your fat, happy seed children.
I still plant lettuce seeds, Buttercrunch,
that came from your serious saving.
Will you fade when the envelope is empty
of life rattling around in seed form?
"Bev's Rapricio"—I see the sign
in another woman's tomato patch,
and in another, and in my own.

We are saving you.

I remember you lovingly each spring, each fall
when it comes time to bury
the morsels of new life you lovingly nurtured
and gave away.

How you loved the soil
How you loved the bugs
How you loved the science
of the cycles
the dormant, the swelling, the opening
push of tender miracle sprout
hungry and thirsty.

How well you fed your progeny
the crowded carrots   the giant mustard leaves
the hot rank summer of lusty success
    the Triumph of Food
Food to share, food to dry, to can
before the shrivel and pucker of pods

where the next generation of seed babies
snuggle down in the cold nursery of winter
to await the next incarnation
while decay enjoys its own feast
and compost works its slow resurrection.

How will I know you when your seed babies are gone?
Yes, there is your great-grandmother's afghan
draped on my couch
and yes, you smile from the photos
    with billowing silver hair
and yes, we recount your brilliance.

But there is nothing quite like
putting your seeds in the ground
legacy of trust in tomorrow
despite the end of your today.

I can keep it going.
The Sweetmeat makes fat seeds every year
I can preserve generations of them.
The Buttercrunch lettuce will stalk up
and flower, and if I am patient,
make tiny seeds to fill the envelope again.

It's not quite the same as being with you
but being with your seeds will do
until it is my turn
to be recycled.
It will keep a trace of you in the palm of my hand
pinch and sprinkle of seeds into the ground.

It will keep me smiling.

Beverly Saves!

Altar Pieces

I

I had the blue jay, dead,
for over a week
a gift to me of feathers, on whole bodied bird.
Reluctant to cut off her arms,
even though her flesh was dead,
I thought of how
a woman's flesh feels on the bones of her wings
as I roll my fingers over her lovingly.
I rolled my fingers lovingly over the shoulders
of the dead blue bird
opened her wings wide, belly down over the white shell altar
in the forest floor clearing.
She was lovely, this blue-petaled creature
I spread her long perfect tail feathers into a narrow fan
She was flight shaped and at her most beautiful.

I have plenty of blue jay feathers,
I said, and pleased myself
with the thought of leaving her whole,
until I noticed her feet.
Black, shriveled skin over shin bones
Sharp-clawed fingers drawn together,
an open fist, frozen just before grab.
Macabre. Exquisite. Crone's feet.
Yes, I must have these.
I do not know why.

I began by twisting both shins at the knee
a pliable dance

 I honor you, I said to her.
 I will not play with you idly:
 May I have your shins and your feet?

70

I decided she would not mind.
I pulled and sawed with my
    thumbnails.
The fibered tendon would not give.
So I walked down the long hill, and back up
    with my sharp pen knife.
Quick, easy—the tough membranes split.

I tucked her sweet curved knobs of femur
    back under soft down,
centered her wingspan over the forest altar
and wished her a blessed journey.
She will not need her feet.
I do not yet know why I do.

II

Tonight I took the two wizened clawed feet
and placed them, open, receiving
on my desk altar
on the delicate pink silk among crystal clusters.
I am praying for something—open, receiving:
It is for wisdom deeper-reaching than the soft flesh
of a woman rolling lovingly under my fingers.
I am going for bone.
I am going for sharp-clawed Death as my Teacher.
    I fit an amethyst into the clutch of one bony foot
    a rose quartz into the grasp of the other.
    Crystal surface hard and bright
    poised against delicate needles of claw
    unpierced jewel cradled by dagger talons.

Now. Teach me again, Mother Death.
How beautiful and instructive are endings.
How bright and adamant is change.
I have been crying for weeks
my lover flown away—quite alive—

feathering her dance without me.
Saw away as I might,
the tough tendon of my sadness holds fast.
My tools are not yet sharp enough
for the clean, releasing cut.
My eyelids are puffed and wrinkled
Gravity of heart pulls on skin.
I watch my face change
And I study shriveled bird skin tight against bird bone.

Ah! The Instruction.
    This heaviness of heart, these falling eyelids
    are only a hint of what will come
    when we all—friends, lovers, crones—
    fly wholly away
    jewels cradled in Death's pointy fingers.
    These love-lost tears
    are slight compared to the life-lost weeping
    we will all cry for each other.
    It is foolish to think there will be less crying
    these decades to come.
    Shrivel and wrinkle and wail are ahead.
    I saw both my robust grandmothers
    shrink into tiny birdwomen, praying for Death.
    I make crystalline bird-footed prayer for the Sharp-Toed Hag
    to remind me
    that lost love is a dry run.

I am comforted, moved by the still life:
these beautiful grave stones, beclawed,
small monuments to certainty,
arrest my pain
startle me in my tearful tracks
insist on deep embrace
of the grim elegance
the shining calm truth of closure.

Praise In Two Voices

I

The Abyss did not win this round.
No, The Unthinkable did not happen
But I am captivated by white-hot wonder:

What If I had not been on that special land
    showing off the brand new solar system that day
What If I had not idly touched the electric cable
    from inverter to battery
Yikes! That Is Hot   That Is TOO Hot!

What If I had not been there to open the battery box
    where wires had melted onto wires
    and patches of plastic insulation had dissolved
    and heat was so intense it broke a metal connector in two
    its former cable floating loose into a drop of plastic jelly.

What Might Have Been is a still-born cataclysm,
apocalyptic horror movie freshly dead
on the cutting room floor

But if all manner of possible universes
co-exist with this one,
then in some other possible realm
the flames do burst out orange and hungry
eat up the cabin
    where archival treasures are gathered round
    this sacred women's land and her forty years
do devour the grasses, the drying brush
race to the meadows, the vast expanse of beige tinder

then up the forested slopes to East and West and North
where giant madrone trees crown
the lofty walls of this precious earth-bowl

terrified critters would run   fly   dig   slither
away from inferno
neighboring woods would blaze conflagration

Loss of life on the land, and beyond
Loss of the land!

I can see down the corridors of disaster
Calamity beyond bearable
I could be haunted by the Nightmare.
I am not.
I am haunted by the Deliverance.

Why?
What force of wanton Grace arranged events just so?
What legion of angels rallied close,
shepherded my footsteps to discovery?
What Deva/Spirit/Beneficent Power guided this story?

Who Are You, O Goddess?
How do I name Thee? — Yes, Thee!
So Holy You are
So magnificent your rescue

I have no ordinary prayer
I bow
for the rest of my life I bow   and marvel
Why do I deserve this mercy?
I was one of the authors of that loose connection
The solar company made their mistake
I made mine
And we would never have known
    the ashes would not have told us why.

The basket of my woman-loving, land-holding arms
    carries a lot
I make room now for this responsibility
The Almost-Catastrophe
And in my Almost-Broken Heart
waves of astounded Praise
rivers of Gratitude earth-core deep
songs of Thanks too full to sing.

The Universe has spoken confirmation:

This Is Holy Work we do
This tendering of land for women and creatures
This Worship of Green
Love of Planet
Adoration of the Mother

All Glory to Her Kindness
Glory Be!

II

Not so fast, Lucky Priestess.
Look again down the hallways of Mystery.
If Pele had not been dissuaded from this feast,
what would your song be?
Lament and sackcloth and oh yes, ashes
Mourning and despair
And Praise? Anyway?
Fierce wrestling with Destiny
screaming fury: This cannot be!

But, in the end, if you play seriously with Surrender,
you cannot pick and choose
    the glorious outcomes.
If you give yourself to Trust
    more radical than circumstance
Your Hallelujah must sound
No matter what.
This is the secret message scribbled
on the backside of event.

Thank you Goddess
    for not forcing my hand
    this time.
May I be ready
    for whatever is delivered
    for whatever searing soaring gift is offered.

Glory Be.
May it be so.

KA-POW! KA-BOOM! CRACK!
O Goddess, What IS Happening?
What shall we do as you slash and burn, Kali-Who-Destroys!
Old structures break open, meltdown inside out
from the stubborn weight of rigid power
Implosion/Explosion. Rubble-rousing-tumult. Truth Quake.
While the Storm Goddesses—Oya, Lilith, Isis—
roar mighty clouds, stir rising seas,
and their brilliant sisters—
Goddesses of Lightning—dance sudden and bright.
Welcome Tian Mu and Mekla, Fulgora and Astrape
Hurling Absolute Change—Illumination!!
Eye of the Storm. Quiet.
Chicken Little and the one hundred monkeys gather in,
expectant, eager to act.
We are in your hands, Kali-Who-Creates
Mother of each nanosecond, when particles glide into wave
and we blink into surprise orbits of energy.
Let there be New. Let us be New.
Let there be Trust in the Never Before.
Let there be Peace in the Always.

Invocation for We'Moon 2016: Quantum Leap Year

World Without End

Kali - The Awakener

Kali: The Awakener D.O.M. Tarot © *Ffiona Morgan 1991*

Oh Moon

Oh Sacred Moon!
Listen up, Blessed One:
This Is Important.

Can you help? Can you somehow ease up on that pulling? The Great Waters here are full of melt. They even upswell warm under the vast expanses of white ice at top and bottom of the otherwise crisp world—and Crack! Break! Tumble! go the frozen rivers into the cresting soup where white bears swim hungry and penguins dive with sunburned feet.

Lady Moon, it is surely not your fault: you play hide and seek like always, but Now the tides you magnet are flooding our edges, and the people are awash in fear, birds and fish awash in plastic crumbles.

It is our fault after all—well, more historically: the patriarchal industrial complex. And we who resist that greed in the name of Love for all our relations—we seek your teachings.

How do you do it? Ride it out in the Dark, and the Light. Keep your cool. Return again and again, Mistress of Certain Change. You are pretty beaten up, from what we can tell. Survivor of who knows what ancient turmoil, your soft light persists and slow bounces to us, percolates through night shadow, time and again and again.

Surely we can learn from your ways of ebb and flow, as we enter this Long Epoch of Earth-Wane. Keep us in your Moon-Wise orbit. Please.

The Disappeared

Hives are empty. Honey bees have gone missing by
the billions There are no mass graves, no sad sodden mounds
of 30,000 dead bees clumped on a hive's bottom board—the
way I found them once, in my beekeeping years, when disease
grabbed them by the fistfuls. No, they are simply gone, from
croplands in countries the world over. Some mysterious
force has spirited them away. Scientists test theories at fever
pitch: A rogue virus? Pesticides? GMO crops? Loss of habitat?
Parasites? Stress? Climate change? Honey bees pollinate ¾
of all flowering plants. Without honey bees, the face of the
planet would be unrecognizable. We would grow hungry for
many foods, and for beauty.

Sweet golden furry ones, where have you gone?
Have you fled into the arms of Melissa,
great bee priestess of Aphrodite?
Has She decreed: "*We won't play any more in the poisoned fields,
with the engineered crops, the toxic orchards. We quit.*"
I see you wild ones
in the rosemary flowers where I live at forest's edge.
You must be hiding out in the woods with Melissa.
You must still do your tail-wagging dances
to tell each other exact coordinates of this flavor flower, that one.
You are a chorus of busy joy,
your specific voice unlike any other insect buzz.

May Melissa tuck you safely into Her vast pollen pockets.
May She nestle you under Her veiled wings
and restore you with the resurrection-magic of honey,
that sacred elixir which once bathed the dead toward eternal life.
May She gather up the billions of you
in a mystery that promises your return
to a world full of glorious blossoms and abundant fruit.
So mote it bee.

Spoils

Blue black oil streaked on dun-colored sand
Rainbow bubbles shimmer petroleum glaze

Sandpipers scamper among toxic morsels
Gulls pluck dinner from poisoned soup

And up among the mastodon logs, I harvest sea-bird bones.
Exuberant vertebrae—tiny beings with their arms flung high
the backbone a stack of joyful postures
each rib a skinny seahorse, each beak a fragile exclamation of face.

I smile and pile my hands high with skeletal whimsy
I will make new creatures from these remains—art of necromancy.

I am dreamy-eyed from the scavenge
I walk along the petroleum froth
the turquoise-colored, lime green, yellow
flecks of plastic vomit at tide line
red bottle caps   brittle white lids
the ugly flood of garbage—regurgitate from careless hominids.
I am embarrassed to be one of this species
arrogant, oil-swigging
oil-slicking children of the massive mother pond.
Matricide.

> She smiles.   Yea, She laughs
> and feathers Her million tidal fingers into the black shore sands
> weaving layers of dark, layers of dun
> herringbone tapestries
> filigree rivulets from dinosaur crumbs
> intricate lace of oil-on-sand.

She has not yet perfected Her design with the plastic splatter.
Of course, it will be stunning. She can make Beauty out of anything.
And who knows
> what species may someday thrive on plastic fodder
> what creatures may someday pluck, exhibit, fuel machines with
> my bones.

Current Events

A small splash of news from the air waves.
I flood with The Absurd.
Let me tell you:
In Bolivia, these days,
it is illegal for people to catch rainwater from their roofs.
   Centuries of rainwater falling into barrels and tubs
   buckets of life falling from the sky
   for crops and herds, baths and drink.
It is illegal now to catch raindrops.
The corporations have bought the water rights.
I told you: Absurd.

In South Asia, corporations copyright pollen.
Seeds that make plants that make seed become contraband.
Generations of botanical care wiped out by company patent.

   Perhaps soon they will sell bottles of sunshine.
   Clouds will wear brand names,
   And if you do not have the price of air,
   you will not breathe.

Greed clutches the planet—sucks her juices
gorges on the fat of the land
bites off more than it can chew
will bloat   will choke   will strangle
on the ferment of Stolen Harvest
on the rising tide of earthwise peoples
   catchers of rain, savers of seed, planters of hope
Let me hope.   Let me hope.

Update:
In Bolivia, these more recent days,
raincatchers rose up like a boiling flood
and swept the Absurd corporation
out of their watershed   out of their country.

Like I told you.

   Stolen Harvest *is the title of a truth-telling book by Vandana Shiva,*
renowned environmental scholar and activist.

Elegy for Benazir Bhutto
Murdered December 27, 2007

Today was a triumph for
the PeopleWhoHateWomen
jihadists: shock troops for misogyny

Color them male
Color them praying
to their male god
Color them proud of assassination
and mayhem.

Yes, they would also have killed her
were she a man
bestirring the people
flouting the powers
espousing the modern
But you and I know
that the PeopleWhoHateWomen
are gleeful in their heart of hearts:
a *woman* who dared be public hero
is wiped out.

Listen up, PeopleWhoAreWomen,
the deed proclaims.
See what happens if you step outside
your sacred family prison
your ordained role as our mother, wife, daughter
Little girls, we burn your schools
and you in them
We stone you for showing an ankle
for having the nerve to be raped
And never, ever imagine
that you could govern a country.

Color me grieving.
She was so beautiful.
Her soft headscarf elegantly, barely draped
Her dark eyes flashing, framed by make-up,
sign of her freedom.
Smart, determined, brave
Flawed: no stranger to shady deals,
foolhardy at times.
But how the PeopleWhoAreJustPeople
loved her
and how she gave them hope!

You and I know
that countless little girls
in their heart of hearts
in their mirrors
will continue to see her face
to say her name
follow her hope.

This time, we also,
PeopleWhoLoveWomen,
have a martyr.

Color us The Future.

Debriefing
From a Goddess of Mesopotamia
During War on Iraq

I know it's not much of a domain any more.
"Queen of Heaven," they used to say.
Queen of rubble and ruin
since wind and armies and centuries
swept my temples to dust.
Once, the Euphrates ran in an old channel
farther to the East.
Some of my great cities—Ur, Kish, Nippur—
were on those forgotten banks
south, east of Babylon.

Oh, let us not forget Babylon.
The Christians are always eager
to settle scores with Babylon,
pummeled though she be already
by Kassites and Hittites, Persians and Greeks.
Poor dust heap,
    hardly the Mother of Harlots any longer
    brick piles on the road to Iraqi Baghdad, war zone.

These herds of armored beasts speeding by
have no idea
Those winged metal birds raining fire
are oblivious
That voice-in-a-box talking of troops at the Tigris
—sacred Tigris—
cannot imagine
Just whose vallied lap
is blasphemed by bullets and bombs
Just whose people, for the first time,
made a wheel go round.

Ancient peoples of the valleys called me
  Nammu, Mother of Heaven and Earth
  Tiamat, Irnini, Nana, Nina, Ninkasi,
  Ninsun, Ninsunna
They named me
  Ninkarrah, Gula, Bau, Ninti, Nintu,
  Nikkal, Ningal, Ninhursag, Ninlil, Lilith
They prayed to me
  Ishara, Aruru, Mami, Nanshe, Ana,
  Anna-Nin, Ama, Inanna, Innin
They honored me
  Akka, Nidaba, Ishtar, Nin Sikil, Gutira,
  Ereshkigal, Nimahor, Ninmah.

They worshipped me in Sumerian/Akkadian cities
now rubbled and buried:
  Lagash, Umma, Khafajah, Agrab, Agade,
  Eshnunna, Al Ubaid, Badtibera, Ur, Kish,
  Nippur, Uruk, Babylon, Calah, Arpachiyah,
  Assur, Arbela, Darahujah, Mari, Ischali, Kissuru,
  Ninevah (near the fighting: Iraqi Mosul),
  Eridu, where river vulva met the mighty gulf
      (near the combat: Iraqi Basra).

Uruk, mighty ancient city, was my jewel.
My temple, E Anna, my House of Heaven.
Holy storehouse where, for the first time,
my priestesses pressed stylus into wet clay,
forming marks to record assignments of land,
allotments of my bounty: wheat and barley,
cattle, fish and fruit.

So many tales of me as Goddess of Love and War.
Yes, I was feisty.
My sons so bloodthirsty. My daughters,
celebrants of sex prayer at holy altars.

Forgotten, though,
    my temples of healing
    the prophecy shrines where priestesses
        spoke dream, gave counsel
    the wayside shrines, Ibratu, for women,
        for daily prayer.
Forgotten, my reverence as
    Giver of law, Judge of polity
    Protector of the weak and the ill
    Mother of writing
    Teacher of grain, of seed and harvest,
        building and craft.

The glories are gone.
The sands soak up memory, and fresh blood.
What's an old goddess to do?
I weep.
I do not need my temples back
I do not need my lion throne.
I need the guns to be stilled.
I need to hear my children laughing
    to see my people eating their fill.
I need for peace to flower
in this dry desert of the human heart.

I weep.

Prayer

Hail Nerthus!
Anti-war Goddess of old
Where are You, Nerthus?
Come.
Come now.
Come running with your red wagon
    bumping over the battlefield.
The battlefields have become supermarkets, restaurants,
    bus stops, refugee camps, churches, temples, mosques
Hurry!
The soldiers have become children.

Just say the word
    and guns will not fire
One glance from You
    grenades will not explode
    bombs will fall flat
Come, with Your holy force field,
    turn landmines into flowers
    into fruits for starving peoples.
Lift one finger, mighty Nerthus,
    and trigger Peace
    monkeywrench the machines of war
    with Your Love
    dull the blade
    catch the missile
    grab the detonator
    pile Your wagon high with dead weapons
    cart them off the edge of earth
    charm bullets into rain for thirsty ground
    magnetize the radar, the laser, the electronic din of killing
    into music for sore hearts.

Easy enough with the hardware.
It is the heart where War has run amok.

Today, a teenage girl became a bomb
blew herself up and innocent others
in the land called Holy
in the land sacred to cousin peoples
who rip into each other
day after vengeful day.

Take her Mother Nerthus,
into Your forgiving arms
Arms, for giving.
Soothe her blasted spirit
tender her grief for brothers, orchards, hopes destroyed
melt her rage into compassion
for those she maimed.

Send her ghost into the dreams of her comrades, her foes
　　to whisper No More!
No More Martyrs.
Let her be an angel
　　of remorse
　　of mercy
Let her haunt with soft soul the hardened hearts
　　of peoples wronged by peoples
　　everywhere.

Goddess! Send us legions of angels
　　to work inner-life miracles
　　with Mercy, irresistible.
Flood the halls of power, the tents of the dispossessed
　　with Mercy
Still with Mercy the command to shoot, bulldoze, launch
Disable with Mercy the instinct to fight
Inspire with Mercy the passion to mend
Pour out Mercy, O Nerthus, to the ends of the earth.

Hurry, Nerthus!
Hurry!

HA! O Queen of Play!
We invoke you with this holy Breath of Life: HA!
Laughter, your gift to us; Joy, your sacrament
Mirth, your flaunt-in-the-face of stern fear:
fear of the underbelly, the belly, the female, the earth.
Come out from Shadow, all you reviled She-demons
Eris, Goddess of Chaos—Lilith, Dark Moon Goddess—
Laverna, Goddess of Rascals.
Kali-Ma, disrupt our demonizing habits
Help us face the Other within, smile into the mirror,
find ally beneath the monster masks—guffaw until we cry?
The deck is stacked, the planet running out of trumps.
Stakes are high, wrongdoing is no joke: How do we deal?
Coyote-woman, Isis, Morrigan—
Show us your shape-shifting tricks of transformation
Khandromas, trickster Dakinis of the rainbow,
Deepen the clever arts of Invention, of Resistance
Flip each day into a new game of unimagined Possibility.
Beguile us from old patterns. Charm us into Change.
She-Who-Jests, crack us up. Crack us Open.
A HA!   Restore the Wild.   A HO!

Invocation for We'Moon 2015: Wild Card

Magic Acts

Aida Wedo © *Hrana Janto 2001*

The Spirit of Theater/The Theater of Spirit

What moves us?
What opens us?
What puts us in touch with Spirit?
    with the cosmos, with the mysteries of Life and Death?
Anything can do that:
    a tree, a cloud, a moth, a song . . . .
Whenever we Open, There is Wonder.

Theater is a way of Opening. Ritual is a way of Opening.
Like the chicken and the egg, which came first? The earliest
ritual was theater; the earliest theater was ritual. Theater in its
origins was always sacred work. A community gathers, creates
sacred space—which is to say, time/place outside ordinary life.
Unlike ritual, which can be performed in solitude, theater most
always happens in a collective context: there are participants and
witnesses. There is opening for the one who performs, there is
opening for the one who witnesses. There is Theater of Release, of
Healing—Catharsis. There is Enactment. Wondrous Enactment.

A Buddhist meditation teacher-friend distinguishes between the
two grand spiritual paths. One is the Path of Emptiness. Quiet.
Contemplation. Meditation. Inwardness, beyond Expressing.
Receiving. Accepting.

The other is the Path of Ecstasy. There are elements of both in
theatrical ritual, but for the most part, Theater belongs to the
Ecstatic traditions.

Enactment.
We Beat the Drums.
We Call In the Gods and Goddesses.
Make a Joyful Noise in the House of the Lord.
Sacred Dance. Sacred Music.
Trance.   Possession.   Channeling.
Being inhabited by Spirits

by archetypes from the Vast Unconscious
by beings in our own Inner Pantheons.
In Theater, as in expressive worship,
We imagine. And most important: we embody what we imagine.
We make up stories about how the world came to be.
We dress up like the Spirits—that's an invitation to be inhabited.
It's easier to do something outrageous when we dress up.

There is Enactment that proclaims itself Holy Theater:
Prophetic Action. Actions like those of Old Testament prophets.
Ezekiel lay on his side for days,
calling the people to repent, with outrageous Enactment.
 Think guerrilla theater.
 Think street theater.
 Think Civil Disobedience.
There is an edge here. Danger.
Danger that conviction can lead to the demonic.
Religious zealotry feeds on enactment that has gone mad.
You can fill in the blanks: madmen in the Middle East
who blaspheme the Goddess Isis with their atrocities;
murderers drunk on the sanctity of unborn life, killing for it.
Does the Great Beyond care?
We imagine She does.
We pretend.

We pretend that we can even speak about the Ineffable.   God?
I invoke the Wisdom of the Path of Emptiness.
I empty into The Beyond.
We can really only point to The Divine.
All we have is metaphor.   And that is Perfect for Theater!
For myself, having trained in theology once upon a Christian past,
my calling is to redress the balance of the last 5000–50,000 years,
when divine metaphor has been occupied by male deity.
It is long past time for Her to take focus. I am Her Priestess.
Theaterwoman, serving the Goddess MetaPhora.
I have enactments for you—In Her Honor.

Rebecca Keaton

[*These are two monologues spoken by Rebecca Keaton, a character
from Bethroot's inner pantheon, first created in 1979. She is
dressed as an odd version of a 19th century country woman, say in
Kentucky or Tennessee: long cotton Sunday dress, leather cowgirl
hat, high top lace-up boots. Her accent is deep country Southern.
She is splitting wood, with full arc swings of a splitting maul. She
splits and talks intermittently.*]

I

Well, whenever I see a sewin' machine, it sets me
to thinkin' about weddin's. Now, that may seem strange to
y'all. But when I was a girl, a weddin' comin' up would put
all the women to sewin'. They'd be sewin' brides' dresses
and bridesmaids' dresses, mother of the bride dresses and
grandmother of the bride dresses, mother of the groom dresses
and grandmother of the groom dresses, and flower girl dresses .
. . there'd be sewin' machines whirrin' night and day all over the
county. Then they'd be stitchin' up weddin' presents. There'd be
hand embroidered dish towels and hand crocheted tablecloths
and hand crocheted place mats. I never saw the likes of such
beautiful work goin' on for such a *sorry* occasion.

I'll tell you about my weddin'. It doesn't have nothin' to
do with sewin', but I'll tell you anyway. My daddy was gonna
perform the ceremony: he and I were talkin' beforehand, and
I said, "Now Daddy, you understand that I can't promise to
obey this man." He said, "But Sugar, it's Scriptural for a woman
to promise to love, honor, and obey her husband." I said, "I
don't care whether it's Scriptural or not. If you put it in there
for me to obey him, then when it comes time for me to say
'Yes, I do'—I'll say 'No, I don't!' and we'll call the whole thing
off right then and there." The old scamp. Actually I'm right
grateful to him. Come time for the ceremony, Daddy said,
"Rebecca Keaton, do you promise to love, honor, and obey this
man?" And I said, "NO, I DON'T!" And I been a free woman
to this day!

II

My Aunt Sophie was somethin' of a preacherwoman herself. They used to say about her, "She was a Prayer Warrior and a Soul Harvester!"

She used to preach about once a month at Sunday night services, and every now and then at revival meetin's. I learned pretty quick that you had to be On Your Toes when it came time for Aunt Sophie to give out the altar call at the end of the service. She'd call on folks to come on down to the altar and give your life over to God, and if you didn't watch out, you'd find yourself marchin' down that aisle, time after time—Aunt Sophie just had this way of pullin' on your heart. She was so compellin', and she could make Heaven seem just as close as this afternoon's banana custard pie—you could just taste it!

We had this new upstart preacher fella from outta-state assigned to the congregation. He got it in his head it was not appropriate for a woman to be preachin', even on occasion. I'm sure he was right jealous of Aunt Sophie, of course. He tried to make it sound all Biblical, about how women were supposed to be quiet and not speak in church. Said "We might as well be Unitarians, havin' a woman in the pulpit."

Well, when Aunt Sophie got wind of what this young man was sayin', she got Fire in her Eye. She went and talked to the Board of Trustees, she talked to the Board of Stewards, she went and talked to the District Superintendent, and she had a long session with the Women's Society of Christian Service. Then one Sunday night, she came and talked to the congregation. I'll never forget it as long as I live.

Brother Harold, that was this fella's name, he had given out the altar call; nobody was comin' down the aisle—and then here come Aunt Sophie walkin' down to the front of the church. She knelt down at the altar for a few minutes. Then she stood up and turned around to face everybody. She had her Bible with her, opened it up, and then she started to talk:

"Brother Harold, all my brethren and sistren: I come down here to this altar tonight to give my life to God as a preacherwoman. I brought my Bible with me. So I'm bringing with me Sarah and Rachel and Rebecca and Hagar and Miriam and Deborah and Mary and Martha and Ester and Ruth and Naomi and Mary Magdalene and Priscilla and Lydia—all the women of faith who fill these pages, and those who've been erased from these pages. That brave Yankee lady Miss Susan B. Anthony put it this way: 'I think women have just as good a right to interpret and twist the Bible to their own advantage as men have twisted and turned it to theirs.'

"The Lord, Bless Her heart, has called me to make a joyful noise in Her House and I will not be shut up. I invite all the women and girls in this congregation who refuse to be silenced in the House of Worship to stand up with me, and shout 'Hallelujah!'"

It was a sight to behold. We were not a shoutin' church, we were a singin' church. But we were a shoutin' church that night. Brother Harold didn't last out the week. Aunt Sophie harvested many a soul, for years to come.

I invite all the women and girls in this congregation who refuse to be silenced in the House of Worship, or Anyplace Else on this Planet, to stand up with me and shout "HALLELUJAH!"

Serpent in the Garden

[Lights go up. We are in ancient time. A paleolithic goddess sculpture is featured in the background. I am crouched underneath an arching branch of curvaceous old wood, tree-like, with a bright red apple sitting on one limb. I am wearing a 4 foot long, 4 inch wide snakeskin, glued to my nose, extending over the top of my head and down the back of my neck. I wear a vest covered with lobes of green and blue velvets and satins—scale-like. A gauzy green and blue cape is around my shoulders. I rapidly flick my tongue up and down, in and out, slowly stretch head and shoulders up, rising to kneel. I am naked from the waist down. Thighs and belly are lightly painted with blue and green scales. My pubic hair is sprinkled lavishly with sequins. I lift my head and "Hsssss" loudly, stretching my neck and turning my head, as snakes do.
I speak very slowly, with long pauses, occasional tongue flickers and hisses. My tone is seductive. My arms stay still at my sides, my hands pressed against my thighs, as though I have no arms.]

I come from the country of Broken Taboo.
Are *you* ever tempted?
I've been watching you.
You must be tired of wearing all those fig leaves.
There are alternatives to living in this—what he calls—"garden."
Hsssssssssss

When Time begins, he will change this story around, of course.
He will want you to think that first you were naked and comfortable with him.
Hsssssssssss

But you are not comfortable.
Come. Just slip out of that old skin.
Doesn't it feel wonderful?
Soft, gleaming new skin of knowing your own body.

I want you to know Everything.
That makes the Rule-maker furious.
He wants all the Power.
He will not want you to remember that
    first, the Power was mine.
In the Beginning was fire and ice and carbon dioxide
And I sat upon the egg of the world.
In the Beginning was fire and ice and methane
And I coiled around the egg of the world.
Here . . . .

[*I bend my head down and bite the apple stem, lift the apple with my teeth, then toss the apple toward the audience, so it rolls on the floor.*]

The egg of the world.

I invite you to be in love with the Earth
    your body, the Earth.
It is against his rules.
So it will be costly.
He will have you suffer and watch much suffering.
It is a brave choice.
Your defiance will show up even in his stories.
You are the first conscious being.
The first to evolve toward choice
    toward Spirit.
I invite you to create the world.

[*I crouch back under the tree arch, down low again. Lights out.*]

Sun Goddess at Summer Solstice

[*Onstage: A replica of Earth, perhaps a large soft exercise ball, or soft sculpture. The Sun Goddess, wearing a bright scarf, enters dancing, connects with and caresses Earth throughout the piece.*]

I am hot. I am blazing hot.
I am 27,000,000 degrees Fahrenheit at center.
I am burning up. I am on fire. I am fire.
I am exploding atoms. I am fusing protons.
I am bursting with energy:
I turn 4 million tons of my mass into energy every second.
I have so much energy:
      If all the water going over Niagara Falls were gasoline, and if that gasoline were burned for 200 million years, it would use up as much energy as I put out in one hour!!

I am intense. I am relentless.
You know me. You feel me. I freckle your white skin.
I burnish your dark skin into deeper shades
of brown and black.
I run rivers of sweat between your breasts.
I warm you. I parch you.
You suck me up with your green leaves.
You drink me into your fibers and cells.
You store me up for eons.
I show you All Beauty, Give you All Life.

      And Today is the Day, my beautiful Earth Daughter, my sweet Earth Sister, my lovely Earth Child—Today is the Day I rope you in. Today is the day I hold on to you—I will not let you spin away. I will not let you fly off into Eternal Light or into Eternal Dark. I pull you back into the cycle. I swing you round again: I'll warm your South, I'll cool your North.
      Today is the Day you *really* know my power. How heavy I am, how enormously attracted you are to me.
      Today is the Day you call me by my names: Akewa Shapas Allat Sun Woman Wurusemu Arinitti Duduhepa

Hebat Nikalmati Asmun Nikal Au Set Isis Amaterasu Omikami Sol Aditi Sunna Sulis Fatima Sekmet . . . To tell the truth, I've been in male drag for about 10,000 years.

[*The Sun sheds Her scarf, puts on a shiny oversized crown, struts about the stage, speaks in deep voice as a male incarnation of the Sun deity.*]

Hup Hup Hup Hup
King! Kill! Fight!! Bright!!
I'm the Bright One!

I'm brighter than all you characters. Use the old noodle: Got myself a fine chariot to ride around the sky! Slick as a whistle. Smooth, shiny. It's got these great golden fins on the rear. Nobody can touch me. The last guy who tried, that fellow Icarus, wound up making candles and stuffing feather pillows with what was left of his gear.
I got everybody beat.

Actually, my rig is in the shop right now. Went a little too fast, overheated. So I'm on foot, as it were.

Hey Ma! How long do I have to keep this up?
[*Arms high as though holding a great ball, bends at the knees, rising up and down many times...*]

Rising and Setting and Rising and Setting . . . .

[*The Sun character shifts back into Sun Goddess but this time wears a bejeweled old fashioned country woman bonnet and affects an irritated old lady voice.*]

That Helios and his machine, trying to steal my fire. Those Ra's-come-lately, what do they know?

You just gotta keep at it with a steady pace. I been doing this for 4.6 billion years, I expect I'll continue for another 5 billion years. Until I explode and then the fragments of you and me and all of us will scatter out there in the universe, and then eventually some of them will coagulate again to make a new star, and we'll start all over again.

I hide my face from you sometimes. Then I hear you

calling out: [*Singing*]
You are my Sunshine, my only Sun, please shine . . .
Now I ask you: Who's gonna make you happy when skies are grey? You counting on someone else to light your fire?

[*Bonnet off, the dancing Sun Goddess with Her bright scarf returns.*]

My Beautiful Earth Woman
I will play with your muscles, your mountains
I will look at my face in your waters
I will dazzle cap you, glisten in a grain of snow
I will touch your lips, your canyon rims

I will hug your belly
Luscious green belt you wear
You will change your garments for me millions of times
I will dapple your forests
Leave my print on your deserts

I will tease you
probe where you open your valleys to me
kiss you all over.
I will Moon over you.
I will change my garments for you millions of times.

[*Sings*]
It is dark in your South now
Long velvet nights to kindle the fire within
And when you see me high in your North sky blooming
Know that the Light changes Dark
changes Light changes Dark.

Mind Play with the Goddess of Wisdom
A Performance Memoir

[*Onstage: A low altar upstage with candle. A backdrop is draped in folds of purple velvet—at its clitoral center a giant rose quartz crystal nestles. A large poof of white taffeta is on the floor to one side. On the other, a small white table is covered by an elegant white cloth laced with gold braid, and holds a white bookstand.*

Bethroot enters, wearing a soft white tunic-like fabric, a headdress of iridescent sparkles and white lace. She carries a long white plumed feather and a large book, bound in white brocaded satin.

She stands centerstage, smiles. Opening the book as if to read, she blows its "words" off the page, and "writes" with the feather plume on its pages and then into the air. She places the open book on the stand, leaves the plume tucked upright into the book.

She moves downstage center and speaks. Gestural movements of hands, arms, body, punctuate her words from time to time: fast finger dance of Shhh at "Silence," scribbling as author, long loud laughter, etc.]

I

I am the body of thought.
I am the sound of mind.
I am the unsound of mind.
I am the daughter of Silence.
Before anything at all existed,
     there was my mother, Silence.

Then She opened her mouth and spoke me.
No one's head split open, She opened her mouth
     and uttered me.
"I have a wonderful idea!" She said.
"I shall have Ideas!" She said.
And so I came to be.
Idea. I, Dea.

Sophia—She who is Wisdom
Tara—Quintessence of Compassion, Illumination

Athena, Metis, Medusa—Triple Goddess of Female Knowing
Hokmah—Spirit of Understanding
Isis—Mother of Magical Knowledge
Maat—She who Wears the Plume of Truth
Afrikete—Goddess of Language and Poems
Sarasvati—Divine Poet, Speaker of Cosmos, of Worlds
Nidaba—Holy Mother of Writing

I am the Author of all life.
I scribble the world—and it is so much fun
    thinking up things!
Sometimes I laugh, and galaxies spill out
    between my teeth.
I blink, and light-years stretch out,
    curl back upon themselves.
I smile, and the universe is a beloved dream.
Sometimes I whisper my secrets to the crystals,
    and they remember.
Some rocks are especially brilliant.
All rocks are wise.
All fibers of being are encoded with my will, my skill.

Sometimes I close my eyes, breathe deeply,
    and invent the circuits of your brain.
You may drink the milk of Wisdom at any time.
I am always available to study with you *what is*.

I mix it up with you: no distant throne in the sky for me
I get into your head,
    we wrestle now and then, we push and pull words
    along the quicksilver folds of your intelligence.

We go deeper than that:
All your thoughts are cells of my body.
All your cells are my thoughts.

Sometimes you close your eyes,
breathe deeply,

and you are one pure moment:
matter and spirit, flesh and heart.

I am the sea you float on.
I am the air of your inner sky.
Your molecules are my dance.
Your soul is the song I sing.
[*singing*] La La La . . .
And when we light the fire
of your imagination together, you and I—
HOLY SMOKE ! ! !

[*A crescendo of sound starts deep with "Holy Smoke" and rises high,
arms are upraised.*]

II

[*Bethroot turns away from the audience, removes her headdress,
listens for a moment to the crystal. She turns the taffeta poof upside
down over her head. It cascades over her shoulders becoming a
billowing evening dress, tiny ruffles upon ruffles of layered nylon
net, a 7 foot diameter circle of swirling fabric. She does not pull the
dress all the way on, leaving taffeta bodice and waistline bunched up
around her neck. Only her head shows, and her legs at mid-calf. She
twirls, the skirt flares out. During the next spoken lines, she postures
with the dress, using hands and arms underneath the fabric: draws it
over her head like a wedding veil, extends arms for an exact semi-
circle, folds it together around her face to make a deep vaginal oval.
She sings a simple lyrical tune:*]

It was 1959. I was valedictorian.
I graduated from high school in this dress.
My mother made it, stitched these tiny ruffles.
And now I read between the seams, it seems to say:

My daughter, I wed you not to a man.
My daughter, I marry you to the power of your own mind
My daughter, serve Sophia,
Seek the brilliance of Woman whole and free.

[*Bethroot swings the skirt around her, speaks with a quick humor.*]
Well, she didn't exactly say that, and I didn't exactly do that. I tried to marry a brilliant man. He said to me, "You know too much." You were Goddam right, Jack—but that's nothing compared to what I know now!!!

I was so smart—I could intuit the answers on exams I had hardly studied for. It was magic! I was a Witch of Good Grades. I wanted them, I got them. I lived by my wits. Summa cum laude. Of course, I never went beyond first semester calculus, and I would not dare physics. Chemistry was my first love.

[*Crouching, emphatic*]
Did you ever watch potassium permanganate crystallize under a microscope?

[*Swinging her arms up high, the skirt becomes a full circle*]
Ohh! Sudden Bright Orange Wonder! I was ecstatic!

[*Drops arms. Matter of fact, ironic*]
So I majored in Religion.
I have a Masters degree entitled Master of Arts in the Comparative Study of Religions (including ChristianThought and History).

[*She pulls a sheaf of white papers from underneath the altar cloth*]

This is my Masters Thesis, written in 1965. I will read to you some of what I wrote. The title is: "Karl Barth's Theology of the Word of God."

[*Reads a few words from many pages—rapidly, sardonically— tossing the pages away one by one as she reads, walking and throwing the papers around the stage.*]

God . . . Man . . . He . . . dialectic . . . man . . . he . . . himself . . . man . . . God . . . kerygmatic . . . his . . . him . . . God . . . Himself . . . facticity . . . he . . . men . . . man . . . prolegomena . . . phenomenologically . . . man . . . him . . . God . . . Father . . . Son . . . his . . . Christology . . . himself . . .

soteriology . . . ecclesiology . . . God Himself . . . he . . . man . . .
trinitarian . . . historicity . . . him . . . He . . . man . . . God . . .
exegesis . . . God God . . . docetic . . .his . . . sanctification . . .
he . . . his . . . God . . . Father . . . Heilsgeschichte . . . man . . .
his . . . Son . . . he . . . men . . . hermaneutics . . . he . . . Himself . . .
paradigmatic . . . God . . . he . . . He . . . himself . . . himself . . .
God . . . men . . . Son . . . he . . . God . . . He God . . . He . . .

[*Finally she throws the papers away in clumps, tosses the whole bunch of them into the air.*]
That's Nothing—compared to what I know now!!

[*She takes the white feather plume, writes in the air, saying:*]
I write it large every day of my life.
SHE! HER!! ME!!

[*Then she goes to the backdrop with the plume, lightly strokes the purple velvet vulva, the pink crystal, tucks the feather at the top of the crystal. She sings passionately, with arms outstretched and skirt wide:*]

Serve Sophia
Seek the brilliance of Woman whole and free.

[*She talks, lifting arms high as the piece ends, as "Holy Smoke" crescendos again, the audience joining, repeat if needed for their participation*]

Sometimes I close my eyes, breathe deeply
and I am one pure moment: matter and spirit,
flesh and heart.
I am the sea I float on.
I am the air of my inner sky.
My molecules are my dance.
My soul is the song I sing.

And when we light the fires of Our imaginations together
You and I . . .
HOLY SMOKE ! ! !

300 sextillion one, 300 sextillion two . . .
O Countless Sky Fires—farther than Eye can see
to the very edge of Light-Travel where Far equals Old,
and it takes you eons to be seen
here where we orbit round your little sister Sun-fire.
We worship the Deep Mystery of your vast Mother Night
Nuit, Ratri, Nott, Itzpapaloti, Ishtar, Nyx
Breksta, give us dreams of the longview Peace
Asteria, divine for us Hope and Healing.
We are your dust, made of your sparkle.
We forget—here in this troubled world.
Help us read your brilliant patterns, connect our distant dots,
navigate the lightways of Compassion.
Bright Star Muses, bring us Song, Art, Story,
Ignite in us passion to create beyond our reach
Open the portals of Imagination
and flame us into revolutionary Grace
I wish I may
embrace your glow
cherish the unknown
I wish I might

Invocation for We'Moon 2017: StarDust

After

Nuit *© Paige Ozma Ashmore 2010*

Artist's Bylines

Deshria is an artist whose work has been internationally published and sold. Twenty years ago, she delved into Shamanism after encountering a chronic illness. Her work is inspired by Irish spirituality, Huna, Folkloric Magic and Animism. She is currently co-creating the *Oracle of the Seer*. Check out her work at deshria.com and oracleoftheseer.com

Ffiona Morgan: Elder Priestess/Lover of Goddess, feminist educator teaches all aspects of the Craft for 43 years; holds rituals/teachings while traveling the world. She visioned and painted Daughters of the Moon. A drummer, artist, writer and well known as a foremother of goddess spirit family. 541-654-0424 or daughtersofthemoon.com

Francene Hart is an internationally recognized visionary artist, and author of *Sacred Geometry Oracle Deck, Sacred Geometry Cards for the Visionary Path, Sacred Geometry of Nature, Sacred Geometry* coloring book. Images of Nature, Spirit and Sacred Geometry. francenehart.com

Hrana Janto: I have long been inspired by mythology, history, fantasy, the natural world and the sacred. Works include: The Goddess Oracle (US Games), book covers, Goddess calendars, children's books and more. To see more, visit hranajanto.com

Leah Marie Dorion is an Indigenous artist from Canada. She loves fire, rivers, animals and children. leahdorion.ca

Paige Ozma Ashmore incorporates ritual and ceremony when making art. Prayers, incantations or blessings cover the canvas before the painting is invoked on it. She specializes in doing intuitive readings through the medium of mixed media art and believes that art is the oldest tool of shamanism other than the drum, which is our own heartbeat. sacredsoulmagic.com/shop

Paula Franco: I am a medicine woman, visual and visionary artist, teacher in sacred art, writer and poet, astrologer, tarot reader, creator of the coloring book *The Ancestral Goddess*. Central to my work is my belief in the healing and transformational power of art—making art fuels human evolution and influences the awakening of global conscience. Learn more at mandalasgoddess.com or email me at pola_astroazul@hotmail.com

Toni Truesdale: Artist, muralist, teacher and illustrator Toni Truesdale celebrates women, the natural environment, and the diversity of the world's cultures. She resides in Biddeford, Maine. Prints and cards are available through website: ToniTruesdale.com. Contact her at tonitruesdale@gmail.com.

Notes and Appreciations

On any given day, I am more likely to be pulling weeds than writing poems, but the Muse sings in my heart with her own special rhythms and revelations. I appreciate all the supportive opportunities that have enabled my work—on the page and/or in performance—to fly. In addition to seven featured Invocations from the We'Moon Datebooks, nine of the poems in this book have been published in We'Moon over the years. The prose piece "Landed" is excerpted from a version published in *Sinister Wisdom* issue #63 "Lesbians and Nature." Two poems—"The Butterfly Effect" and "Altar Pieces"—come from my poetry chapbook published in 1990: *Under the HeartStone*. Several performance pieces are published in this book, either in full—*Serpent in the Garden; Sun Goddess at Summer Solstice; Mind Play with the Goddess of Wisdom*—or excerpted—*Feathers in My Mind: A Very Tale; Rebecca Keaton*.

I am forever grateful to my writerly friends in the Southern Oregon Women Writers' Group, Gourmet Eating Society and Chorus (founded in 1981) for their careful attention to my writings for decades: their critical observations and encouragement, the word-tussles, the brilliant imaginings we polish. Good counsel and helpful feedback for this book came especially from Hawk Madrone, Helen Laurence and H. Ní Aódagaín.

Goddess Fortuna has gifted me with the exquisite pleasure of an actual job working with the creative source material for We'Moon Datebooks, and my colleagues are a dream team: committed, inventive, funny, efficient. Their best efforts have made this book possible. Barb Dickinson is a brilliant editor who conjures words and shapes text with aplomb and eager imagining. Sequoia Watterson is the magician who waves her wands of color and design, and Voila! the images become radiant; artistry of the page takes unique shape. Sue Burns, often busy with numbers and budgets, is herself a word witch and brought enthusiastic wisdom to her review of these pages.

This circle of appreciation embraces Musawa, founder of We'Moon, who had the vision and tenacity to create a publishing company in service to Spirit's work in the world among and through women.

Many thanks to Carolyn Gage and Sandy Boucher who offered gracious advanced praise for this collection. Visit their websites here: carolyngage.com and sandyboucher.info